Featherstone

TIME TO...
MOVE

**Physical Development in the
Early Years: How to observe,
assess and plan for progress**

TRUDI FITZHENRY
AND KAREN MURPHY

Bloomsbury is a registered trademark of Bloomsbury Publishing Plc

First published 2014

British Library Cataloguing-in-Publication Data
A catalogue record for this book is available from the British Library.

ISBN:
PB 978-1-4729-0950-3
ePDF 978-1-4729-1883-3

Library of Congress Cataloging-in-Publication Data
A catalog record for this book is available from the Library of Congress.

10 9 8 7 6 5 4 3 2 1

Printed and bound in India by Replika Press Pvt Ltd.

This book is produced using paper that is made from wood grown in managed, sustainable forests. It is natural, renewable and recyclable. The logging and manufacturing processes conform to the environmental regulations of the country of origin.

To view more of our titles please visit www.bloomsbury.com

Contents

Introduction... 4
How to use this book 5

Chapter 1
0 – 11 months... 6

Chapter 2
8 – 20 months... 20

Chapter 3
16 – 26 months... 34

Chapter 4
22 – 36 months... 40

Chapter 5
30 – 50 months... 54

Chapter 6
40 – 60+ months... 68

Appendix 87
Songs and rhymes 88
Glossary 93
Bibliography 96

Introduction

This is a book about the prime area of Physical Development in the Early Years, and more specifically about Moving and Handling. It is designed for practitioners to use in settings as an assessment tool and guide as they observe and support children's early physical development.

With the revision of the Early Years Foundation Stage (EYFS) in September 2012, Physical Development became a prime area of learning and as such a statutory requirement for all children aged 0-5 years:

> *'The prime areas begin to develop quickly in response to relationships and experiences, and run through and support learning in all other areas. The prime areas continue to be fundamental throughout the EYFS.'*
> **(EYFS Framework 2012)**

The Statutory Framework for the Early Years Foundation Stage applies to all children aged 0-5 years who attend private, voluntary, independent settings, child minders, maintained schools or nurseries and academies. This book seeks to provide valuable guidance for practitioners across the entire Early Years provision. It aims to clarify and expand on ideas to support a child in each phase of development, with links to the EYFS framework. The main objective is to provide a practical tool to enable practitioners to fulfil their statutory duties in an exciting and innovative way.

> *'Physical Development involves providing opportunities for young children to be active and interactive; and to develop their co-ordination, control, and movement. Children must also be helped to understand the importance of physical activity, and to make healthy choices in relation to food.'*
> **(EYFS Framework 2012)**

This book focuses solely on the Moving and Handling aspect of Physical Development in the EYFS because it underpins much of a child's later educational advancement. Without good coordination, core stability and gross motor skills, the fine motor skills needed for tool handling and writing will not fully develop. Each aspect of Physical Development is interlinked with the child's future success as a learner.

If the child is not achieving the development pointer within the given range, practitioners should continue to provide additional appropriate opportunities for the child to become successful. They should discuss their concerns with the child's parents, asking about how the child responds at home and whether they or the child's health visitor or G.P have any concerns. If little progress is made, it may be advisable to request parental permission to seek advice from outside agencies.

How to use this book

This book supports the planning cycle at each stage of development. It contains clear guidance on what to observe, how to assess what is seen through both the assessment notes and progress checklists. Practical ideas to use in planning each child's individual next steps are also provided.

It is intended that the progress checklists could also be used alongside a setting's current tracking system to highlight any areas of concern and demonstrate progress made. It is important that practitioners are aware of their responsibility to encourage parents to contact their health professional if the child appears to be developing outside of the normative range. If there is little or no progress after they have spoken to parents and included timed specific interventions in the child's individual plan, then practitioners should seek parental permission to involve outside agencies.

This book contains practical, easy to follow suggestions linked to the ages and stages of the Early Years Outcomes and offers clear information on what to look for in terms of Physical Development and how to plan for next steps.

Each chapter is linked to a phase or stage of development from birth to 60+ months. Each section is colour coded and links the Early Years Outcomes to the planning cycle, including observations, assessments and planning. Also included are possible links to the Characteristics of Effective Learning.

There are additional activities that offer the busy practitioner a wealth of ideas to choose from linked to that specific age and stage of development. A short glossary features in each chapter and defines key terms as they appear. These definitions explain how we intend the words and phrases to be interpreted within the book. A traditional alphabetical glossary of all terms used appears at the back of the book for quick reference.

The progress checklists at the end of each chapter are available for practitioners to use when observing children's Physical Development. They can be used to demonstrate progress in a specific area over time. The progress checklist at 40 – 60+ months is closely linked to the Early Learning Goal (ELG). It can be used to support the practitioner's professional judgement as to whether a child is at emerging, expected or exceeding level at the end of the Foundation Stage.

TIME TO MOVE

Early Years Outcomes

Turns head in response to sounds and sights.

Gradually develops ability to hold up own head.

Links to the Characteristics of Effective Learning

PLAYING AND EXPLORING

Finding out and exploring

★ showing curiosity about objects, events and people

★ using senses to explore the world around them

Being willing to 'have a go'

★ showing a 'can do' attitude

e.g. the child tries to lift their head in response to a new and interesting sound, even though it is difficult. It is important that the child receives praise and encouragement for this characteristic to develop and persist.

ACTIVE LEARNING

Keeping on trying

★ persisting with activity when challenges occur

Enjoying achieving what they set out to do

★ showing satisfaction in meeting their own goals

e.g. the child keeps trying to hold up their head even though muscles may tire easily. It is important for the practitioner to use their professional judgement to decide how much support to give a child to encourage persistence and help them achieve the personal satisfaction of success.

By 6 months most children turn their heads towards the sound of a familiar voice

TURNS HEAD

HOLDS UP HEAD

Observation
What you may notice…

Does the child turn their head in response to different sounds?

Do they turn their head in response to different **visual stimuli**?

Can they follow a moving object or person with their eyes?

Does the child attempt to lift their head e.g. when being held on your shoulder?

Does the child keep trying to lift their head and increase the length of time they are successful?

Assessment
What it may signify…

The child is able to hear, **mentally process** and respond to a range of sounds. If the child does not respond, speak to parents.*
Find out:

- How the child responds to sounds at home;

- Whether the parents have any concerns;

- What hearing checks the child has already had, if any.

The child is able to see, **mentally process** and respond to sight and movement. If there is little or no response, speak to parents.*
Find out:

- How the child responds at home;

- Do they feel there is a need for a sight check?

- Are there any underlying physical reasons that may restrict movement of the head?

The child's neck muscles are gaining strength at an appropriate rate. If the child does not attempt to lift their head, speak to parents.*
Ask them:

- Can the child lift their head for a short time?

- When does the child attempt to lift their head?

- Are there any underlying physical reasons that may restrict movement of the head?

*If the parents express any concerns about their child's development, encourage them to speak to their health visitor or medical practitioner.

Planning
What you can do...

This links to sections 1 and 2 of the Progress Checklist on p19.

Provide a good selection of resources that offer a range of **pitch** and **volume** e.g. rattles and shakers, rain makers, sleigh bells, musical mobiles and your own voice.

By 3 months most children are moving their head in response to audible stimuli.

Provide a good selection of visually stimulating resources that can be used to encourage **eye tracking** and head movement e.g. moving musical mobiles or light projectors, puppets or toys, objects that sparkle and catch the light. Remember to allow time. The child needs to hear the sound, move their eyes and then their head. Build up the length of activitiy gradually as initially this takes a lot of effort.

Provide a good selection of visually stimulating resources that can be used to encourage lifting and holding of the head e.g. mirrors, colour changing bubble tubes, fibre optic lights or favourite toys.

Position a child-proof mirror in front of the child when they are lying on their tummy to encourage lifting and holding of the head.

By 1 month most children are attempting to lift their head when lying on their tummy.

Additional activities

These are additional activities to further support this stage of development.

Here comes the buzzy bee
(child on your knee or on their back)

With the child lying on their back or sitting cradled by practitioner, slowly move a brightly coloured, large bumble bee toy into and out of sight whilst making buzzing sounds, changing the **pitch and volume** of your voice.

Here comes the buzzy bee, buzz, buzz, buzz.
(fly the bee into sight from left to right)

Where is the buzzy bee? Buzz, buzz, buzz.
(fly the bee out of sight, repeat from other directions and as often from both sides as child remains interested).

By 6 months most children chuckle and laugh when stimulated.

Here comes the buzzy bee
(child on their tummy)

With the child lying on their tummy and the practioner, facing them at their level.

Here comes the buzzy bee, buzz, buzz, buzz.
(fly the bee towards the child and upwards slightly)

Where is the buzzy bee? Buzz, buzz, buzz.
(fly the bee out of sight, repeat flying downwards and away from the child as often as the interest remains).

Moving peek-a-boo

First the practitioner remains in one place to establish the game. They cover their face with both hands then remove them, smiling and saying 'peek–a–boo!' in a sing-song voice. Next, the practitioner peeks out but from a different position, to the left or right, above or below their hands before physically moving to the left or right, or up or down. Repeat to encourage **eye tracking** and head movement.

Look at me

The key person lies or sits opposite the child, at their level, and uses voice and facial expressions to encourage lifting of the head.

Glossary of terms

Visual stimuli: something that provokes a response from the eyes e.g. a picture, toy, object or person.

Mentally process: to think things through.

Head righting reflex: when the head is not in upright position this reflex stimulates appropriate muscles to bring it back into an upright position.

Pitch: how high or low a musical note or sound is.

Volume: how loud or quiet a musical note or sound is.

Eye tracking: the movement of the eyes when following an object.

Early Years Outcomes

Makes movements with arms and legs which gradually become more controlled.

Watches and explores hands and feet, e.g. when lying on back lifts leg to vertical position and grasps feet.

Reaches out for, touches and begins to hold objects.

Links to the Characteristics of Effective Learning

PLAYING AND EXPLORING

Finding out and exploring

★ showing curiosity about objects, events and people

★ using senses to explore the world around them

★ engaging in open-ended activity

★ showing particular interests

e.g. the child grabs their feet and then sucks their toes using sensory exploration to learn about themselves.

ACTIVE LEARNING

Being involved and concentrating

★ showing high levels of energy, fascination

★ paying attention to details

e.g. when stimulated by an object, sound or person of interest the child moves their arms and legs rapidly. It is important that practitioners provide positive feedback through smiles, gestures, speech and repetition to encourage and develop the child's interest and focus.

ARMS AND LEGS

HANDS AND FEET

REACHES OUT

Observation
What you may notice...

Does the child show a willingness to move their arms and legs freely?

Does the child appear to have limited ability to move their arms and legs?

Does the child show an interest in their hands and feet?

Can the child grasp their own feet?

Does the child grasp tightly onto an object or finger, when it is placed in their hand?

Does the child reach out for and touch objects?

Does the child hold some objects?

Assessment
What it may signify...

The child is developing **muscle tone** and strength in their arms and legs.

If the child does not move their legs and arms freely there may be a lack of **muscle tone** and strength. Speak to their parents.* Find out:

- What is the child's usual range of movement?

- Are there any underlying physical reasons for their restricted movements?

The child is developing an interest in themselves and an awareness of **proprioceptive feedback**. Lack of interest may be due to lack of stimulation by adults, or an inability to focus the eyes or follow objects with the eyes. If the child doesn't respond to visual stimulation, speak to their parents.* Find out:

- How does the child respond to visual stimulation at home?

- Do the parents have any concerns about the child's vision?

If the child can grasp their feet, they are developing and increasing their **core strength**, which is essential for creeping and crawling. If the child can grasp other objects but not their feet, practitioners should consult parents* to see if there are any physical restrictions to the child's movement.

This may show the presence of the **palmer reflex**.

The child is developing an interest in the world around them. The **asymmetrical tonic neck reflex (ATNR)** is working to increase muscle tone and hand-eye coordination.

The child is gaining some control of their hand movements and grasp.

*If the parents express any concerns about their child's development, encourage them to speak to their health visitor or medical practitioner

Planning
What you can do...

This links to sections 3,4 and 5 of the Progress Checklist on p19.

Encourage a variety of movements through smiling and praising the child's efforts.

Support different ways of moving by tapping feet together; clapping hands together and providing a resistant surface (such as your hand) for them to push against. This will provide **proprioceptive feedback**.

Provide opportunities for babies to kick, wave arms and move freely on their back and their front, both indoors and outdoors e.g. on a play mat, on grass or in a paddling pool under constant supervision.

Encourage exploration of hands and feet. Play games and sing rhymes involving fingers and toes such as *This Little Piggy*.

Tap the child's hands together, then feet together, then hands and feet together, remembering to add positive facial expressions and interesting sounds while doing it.

Place your finger or other suitable object into the child's hand for them to grasp. Encourage the child to release the object by gently moving the object.

Ensure that a wide range of objects (some that move or make sounds when touched) are placed within sight and reach.

Move favourite objects, or ones that make sounds, slowly in different directions but within the **visual midfield** for short periods of time.

By 6 months most children are able to reach, grasp objects and pass between hands.

Additional activities

These are additional activities to further support this stage of development.

Mobiles and lights

Suspend or position mobiles or colour-changing lights directly above a cot or mat to encourage arm and leg movement.

Place or suspend toys that make a noise or change colour when touched, within reach of hands and feet.

Provide a range of black, white and red coloured objects and books to stimulate interest.

Baby massage

Gently massage the child's arms, legs and body to develop a sense of **proprioceptive feedback**.

Free feet

Whenever possible allow children to have bare feet for increased sensitivity and **proprioceptive feedback**.

Musical feet

Place a foot piano within reach of the child's feet to encourage repeated movements.

Fingers and toes

Play games and sing rhymes involving fingers and toes such as *1, 2, 3, 4, 5* and *This Little Piggy*.

Fancy hands and feet

Attach baby wrist rattles to wrists or ankles to encourage movement and grasp.

Round and Round the Garden

Round and round the garden like a teddy bear (practitioner sits child on their lap and they hold one of the child's hand palm up and trace circles on it); *one step* (practitioner moves their hand to the crook of the child's elbow); *two steps* (practitioner moves their hand to the child's armpit; *tickle him/her under there!* (practitioner tickles the child).

Glossary of terms

Muscle tone: an unconscious low level contraction of muscles at rest.

Proprioceptive feedback: sensory feedback that tells us where our body parts are in space without having to look e.g. being able to put an object into our mouth. It also helps us to know how much force we need to use to do something e.g. how hard to grip something without squashing it or how to throw a ball so that it goes far enough but not too far. Activities involving resistance give us the most feedback.

Core strength: the ability to use tummy and back muscles in a balanced way.

Asymmetrical tonic neck reflex (ATNR): this is a primitive reflex usually present up to 6 months. It is seen when the child is lying on their back and their head is turned to one side. On the same side that the head is facing, the arm should reach out and the leg straighten. The arm and leg on the opposite side should bend. This is sometimes known as the 'fencer' position.

Palmer reflex: a primitive reflex which uses the muscles of the hand and supports the development of fine motor control.

Visual midfield: the area that both eyes can see at the same time.

Palmer grip/grasp: using the whole hand to hold onto and use objects.

Early Years Outcomes

Rolls over from front to back and from back to front.

When lying on tummy becomes able to lift first head and then chest, supporting self with forearms and then straight arms.

Explores objects with mouth, often picking up an object and holding it to mouth.

Links to the Characteristics of Effective Learning

PLAYING AND EXPLORING

Finding out and exploring

★ showing curiosity about objects, events and people

★ using senses to explore the world around them

★ engaging in open-ended activity

e.g. the child finds out about the properties of objects by placing them in their mouth: are they hard or soft, warm or cold, rough or smooth? It is important to provide a wide variety of safe objects for exploration and ensure the child is supervised and all choking hazards are well out of reach.

ACTIVE LEARNING

Being involved and concentrating

★ paying attention to details

Keeping on trying

★ persisting with an activity when challenges occur

e.g. the child can see their favourite toy or person just out of reach. As they keep on trying to stretch towards it they roll over. As they practice this new skill they come to realise that it enables them to move around and explore their world.

CREATING AND THINKING CRITICALLY

Having their own ideas

★ finding new ways to do things

Making links

★ making links and noticing patterns in their experience

e.g. the child rolls from their back onto their right side when reaching for a toy placed to their right. In time, they start to use their arms to reach and roll over to explore this new movement.

	Observation What you may notice...		Assessment What it may signify...
ROLLS	Can the child roll from front to back?	▶	The child is developing an interest in the world around them and beginning to develop their **core strength**.
	Can the child roll from back to front?	▶	If the child cannot roll or shows no interest in rolling, this may be due to a lack of stimulation in the environment or by adults. Speak to parents.* Find out: • Does the child roll or attempt to roll at home? • When does the child do this?
TUMMY TIME	Does the child lift their head when lying on their tummy?	▶	If the child can lift their head when lying on their tummy, their neck muscles are gaining strength. The child may be developing an interest in their surroundings.
	Does the child lift their chest when lying on their tummy, supported by their forearms?	▶	If the child can lift their chest and head when lying on their tummy, they may be developing their upper body strength. If the child shows no interest in lifting their head or chest this may be due to lack of stimulation in the environment or by adults. Speak to parents.* Find out: • Does the child lift their head or chest at home? • When does the child do this?
EXPLORES WITH MOUTH	Does the child show a willingness to explore objects with their mouth?	▶	The child may be developing an interest in **sensory exploration**. If the child shows no interest in exploring objects with their mouth, check they are not being discouraged by the presence of a dummy or lack of encouragement to do so. Speak to parents.* Find out: • Does the child mouth objects at home? • Does the child have favourite objects or textures at home?

Planning
What you can do...

This links to sections 6, 7 and 8 of the Progress Checklist on p19.

Encourage the child to reach first then roll – place favourite objects to the side within the child's sight but just out of reach, gradually moving them further until rolling is achieved.

Play rolling games such as *Ten in the bed* with the adult, rolling the child to support **proprioceptive feedback** and a feeling of movement.

Most children are able to roll from front to back by 5-6 months.

Provide plenty of opportunities for floor play with the child on their tummy. Keep the sessions short but interesting, gradually increasing the time as the child gains more strength and control.

The key person lies or sits opposite the child and uses their voice, facial expression and favourite objects to encourage lifting of the head and chest.

Most children are able to lift head and chest when lying on their tummy. Arms may be extended and used for support with palms flat on the floor by 4-8 months.

Provide a wide range of interesting, yet safe, objects for the child to explore with their mouth e.g. wooden spoons, teething rings, edges of soft comforters, plastic keys etc. Make sure objects are large enough not to be swallowed and supervise the child during play.

Ensure that objects for mouthing offer different textures and temperatures (room, slightly chilled — but not too hot or cold).

Most children explore objects with their mouth by 6 months.

Additional activities

These are additional activities to further support this stage of development.

Make the bed

Make the bed – wrap the child tightly in a blanket or piece of lycra stretchy material. The child needs to be able to support their own head before engaging in this activity

Shake the bed – pat and jiggle the child within the blanket or lycra.

Turn the blanket over – roll the child from the blanket or lycra.

Heads up

When the child is on their tummy, gently place a hand on the child's bottom – this helps them to lift their head. Initially expect one lift of the head and increase gradually.

Exploring textures

Lie the child on their tummy on different textures e.g. a fleecy blanket, carpet, the grass, silky material, velvet, play mats, pat mats (water filled).

Glossary of terms

Core strength: the ability to use tummy and back muscles in a balanced way.

Sensory exploration: using the senses (in this case the mouth) to make sense of the world.

Proprioceptive feedback: sensory feedback that tells us where our body parts are in space without having to look e.g. being able to put an object into our mouth. It also helps us to know how much force we need to use to do something, e.g. how hard to grip something without squashing it or how to throw a ball so that it goes far enough but not too far. Activities involving resistance give us the most feedback.

Progress Checklist: 0 – 11 months

Name ....

Date						
Age in months						

Use different coloured pens to track assessments so that progress can be seen.
Tick 'yes' if the child is fully able to perform the movement.
Tick 'some difficulty' if the child can sometimes perform the movement but not easily.
Tick 'severe difficulty' if the child rarely or never performs the movement.

		Yes	Some difficulty	Severe difficulty
1a	Turns head in response to different sounds.			
1b	Turns head when name is called – normal voice.			
1c	Turns head when name is called – whisper.			
1d	Turns head in response to slowly moving brightly coloured objects.			
1e	Turns head in response to different sights.			
2a	When lying on front able to raise head momentarily.			
2b	Able to hold head upright for a few seconds when being held.			
3a	Able to bend and stretch arms simultaneously.			
3b	Able to 'bounce' using legs to push off when held for support.			
4a	Shows a fascination for own hands and/or feet.			
4b	When lying on back able to grasp feet.			
4c	Able to bring hands together when playing with them.			
5a	Able to close hand tightly for a few seconds when practitioner's finger (or suitable object) is placed on child's palm.			
5b	Able to track a slow moving object.			
5c	Able to reach for and grasp objects.			
6a	Able to roll from front to back.			
6b	Able to roll from back to front.			
7a	Able to lift head when lying on tummy.			
7b	Able to lift chest when lying on tummy.			
8a	Able to grasp an object and put in mouth.			

Time to Move © Karen Murphy and Trudi Fitzhenry, published by Featherstone 2014

8 – 20 months

Early Years Outcomes

Sits unsupported on the floor.

When sitting, can lean forward to pick up small toys.

Pulls to standing, holding on to furniture or person for support.

Links to the Characteristics of Effective Learning

PLAYING AND EXPLORING

Finding out and exploring

★ showing curiosity about objects

★ using senses to explore the world around them

★ engaging in open-ended activity

★ showing particular interests

Being willing to 'have a go'

★ initiating activities

★ seeking challenge

★ showing a 'can do' attitude

★ taking a risk, engaging in new experiences, learning by trial and error

e.g. the child learns through trial and error just how far they can lean without falling over when reaching for or grasping objects of interest, which they explore with touch, sight or taste.

ACTIVE LEARNING

Being involved and concentrating

★ maintaining focus on their activity for a period of time

★ showing high levels of energy, fascination

★ paying attention to details

Keeping on trying

★ persisting with an activity when challenges occur

★ bouncing back after difficulties

e.g. the child continues to try and pull up on furniture and stable equipment in order to see or touch an object of interest even though it may take many attempts. Practitioners need to provide new and stimulating resources and intervene with support if the child is becoming frustrated.

8 – 20 months

SITS

LEANS

PULLS TO STANDING

Observation **What you may notice...**		Assessment **What it may signify...**
Can the child sit unsupported?	▶	The child is developing **core stability**.
Does the child appear fretful or anxious when sitting unsupported?	▶	The child lacks **core stability** or has a fear of falling or collapsing.
Can the child lean or move towards and grasp objects?	▶	The child is developing core stability and the child's **palmer reflex** is **integrating**.
Does the child choose to lean or move towards and grasp objects to either side?	▶	The child is not motivated to move because the environment lacks stimulation.
Can the child use stable objects such as furniture to pull to standing?	▶	The child is developing strength in arms, an interest in their environment and desire to move.
Does the child infrequently use stable objects such as furniture to pull to standing?	▶	The child lacks muscle strength in arms, an unstimulating environment or encouragement to move.

By 12 months most children are able to pull themselves to standing.

Planning
What you can do...

This links to sections 1, 2 and 3 of the Progress Checklist on p33.

Sit with the child on the floor facing you and support them between your legs. Gently rock them back and forth and from side to side whilst encouraging them to try and hold themselves. Use smiling facial expressions and sing a rhyme such as *Rock-a-bye baby*.

Surround the child with cushions or pillow so they feel the support at their back and sides and have a soft landing should they fall.

Provide a wide range of exciting physical activities that encourage rolling, rocking, travelling (child's choice to crawl, shuffle, roll or develop own method) and balancing with adult support as necessary. All of these support the development of core stability.

To integrate the **palmer reflex** and strengthen hand muscles, provide a range of textures and consistencies such as dough, lycra, **gloop**, sand and earth, and encourage exploration including stretching, pulling, stirring, digging, and spreading with hands.

Provide low level, stable furniture that will support the pulling up process without wobbling.

Provide **muscle resistant play** that involves pulling and pushing e.g. *See Saw Margery Daw* or similar rocking activities where the child is using their hands and arms to pull forward and lean back.

Ensure the environment is well planned and includes a range of new, interesting and familiar or favourite objects to encourage the desire to pull to standing and move.

Additional activities

These are additional activities to further support this stage of development.

Row your boat

Sit the child on your knees facing you, holding on to their arms. Gently rock them backwards and forwards whilst singing the song.

My favourite things

To encourage movement towards things (by leaning, rolling, crawling, or pulling up), identify what interests or attracts the child's attention (a favourite toy, bright colours, moving object or interesting sounds. Attract the child's attention and then place the object slightly out of reach in front, then slightly to the left then right. Reward attempts to reach or successful grasping with praise and encouragement, gradually increasing the distance from the child.

Squeezy time

To strengthen hand muscles use a range of sponges (different shapes and sizes), both dry and wet, and encourage squeezing, wringing and twisting movements.

Hand massage

Gently squeeze along each finger and thumb, front and back, side to side, holding at the tip. Do this to encourage the child's use of fingers to explore their environment.

Out for fun

Review your outdoor environment. Is there a range of sturdy low level equipment, such as climbing frames, benches, raised beds, sand and water trays, for small children to experiment with pulling up to standing.

Round and round the garden

Chant this rhyme whilst gently pressing on the child's palm to stimulate hand muscles.

Bouncing fun

Sing *Horsey, Horsey,* gently bouncing the child on your knee to develop **core stability**.

Flying high

Challenge the child's core stability by holding them upright **horizontally** while 'flying' them around.

Glossary of terms

Core stability: the muscle group (including abdominals) responsible for stabilising the body and supporting posture.

Palmer reflex: a primitive reflex that curls the fingers when the palm of the hand is tickled, also known as the 'grasp' reflex. This reflex exercises the hand muscles and supports fine motor control.

Integrating: when the reflex is serving its purpose in supporting an area of development.

Muscle resistant play: heavy work and proprioceptive play activities that provide resistance so that muscle strength is developed.

Gloop: corn flour and water mixed to varying consistencies.

Horizontally: relating to the horizon, e.g. a line going from left to right.

Early Years Outcomes

Crawls, bottom shuffles or rolls continuously to move around.

Walks around furniture lifting one foot and stepping sideways (cruising), and walks with one or both hands held by an adult.

Takes first few steps independently.

Links to the Characteristics of Effective Learning

PLAYING AND EXPLORING

Finding out and exploring

★ showing curiosity about objects, events and people

★ showing particular interests

Being willing to 'have a go'

★ initiating activities

★ seeking challenge

★ showing a 'can do' attitude

★ taking a risk, engaging in new experiences, and learning by trial and error

e.g. the child's curiosity about objects, events and people provides the impetus to find new ways to move around.

ACTIVE LEARNING

Keeping on trying

★ persisting with activity when challenges occur

★ bouncing back after difficulties

Enjoying achieving what they set out to do

★ showing satisfaction in meeting their goals

★ enjoying meeting challenges for their own sake rather than external rewards or praise

e.g. once the child is able to roll at will they may choose to do so purely to experience the pleasure of movement, changing direction when they meet immovable objects then rolling again.

CREATING AND THINKING CRITICALLY

Having their own ideas

★ finding new ways to do things

Choosing ways to do things

★ changing strategy as needed

e.g. whilst cruising round furniture towards an encouraging practitioner the child may need to stop, lower themselves and crawl, shuffle and roll to reach the person or object of interest.

CRAWLS, SHUFFLES, ROLLS

WALKS WITH SUPPORT

FIRST STEPS

Observation
What you may notice...

Can the child creep, crawl, shuffle or roll?

Does the child appear motivated to move around?

Can the child walk around furniture (cruise)?

Does the child walk with one or both hands held by an adult?

Can the child walk independently (a few steps)?

Does the child appear reluctant to demonstrate a desire to walk unsupported?

Assessment
What it may signify...

The child's **Symmetrical Tonic Neck Reflex (STNR)** is becoming **integrated.**

Lack of stimulation from adults and/or the environment may suppress the child's natural desire to move and explore.

The child's **core strength** is developing.

The child is developing their natural desire to explore the world around them.

The child is developing their natural desire to explore the world around them.

The child may have a fear of falling.

Most children are able to take some independent steps by 17 months.

Planning
What you can do...

This links to sections 4, 5 and 6 of the Progress Checklist on p33.

For reluctant crawlers ensure children are given plenty of time on their tummies (start with 1-2 minutes and gradually increase), this not only encourages crawling but supports integration of the **STNR.**

Provide novel and interesting items and activities that catch the attention and interest of children, encouraging them to seek to explore both indoors and outside and develop their **gross motor skills.**

Place interesting items on top of furniture to encourage pulling up and cruising.

Place stable items of furniture close together but not touching to encourage reaching and first steps.

Crawling is often established by 12 months.

Ensure plenty of opportunities to explore in a safe environment such as on soft play surfaces with a range of large soft play equipment that includes slopes, low level steps and tunnels.

For children that are reluctant walkers, ensure that adults offer physical support and encourage all attempts with smiles and gentle voices.

Additional activities

These are additional activities to further support this stage of development.

Roly poly

When a baby is lying on their back, sit behind them, holding a small toy over their head. Once you have their attention, move the toy very slowly to one side, all the while encouraging the baby to get it. If they roll over, present them with the toy. You can repeat the game on the other side.

Sausage rolls

Roll an ordinary bathroom towel into a 'sausage'. Gently position the 'sausage' under the child's upper body, with their arms hanging over the front. The towel 'sausage' supports the upper body – NOT the stomach – with the elbows just touching the carpet. It should slightly raise the upper body thereby allowing the child to discover their surroundings. Make sure the child's elbows touch the carpet - they must not be hanging in the air. Get down on the floor directly in front of the child and face them. Now, let the child look at your face while you talk to, amuse and encourage them.

Crawling confidence

Sit down on the floor and stretch your legs out in front of you. Lay the child on their tummy across your legs (arms and upper body on one side of your legs, their legs on the other) and support them. In this position, the child should be in the natural crawling stance and it forces them to carry some weight on both arms and knees, thereby strengthening at the same time. Once the arms and legs become stronger, crawling should come naturally.

Push-off

Place the palms of your hands behind the child's feet when they are on all fours. This stabilises them and gives them something to push off from when they are just learning to crawl.

Push-along-toys

Provide different push-along toys for the child to use to support themselves when attempting to walk. Use large balance balls, with an adult supporting the opposite side, to provide resistance and stability.

Glossary of terms

Core stability: the muscle group (including abdominals) responsible for stabilising the body and supporting posture.

Symmetrical Tonic Neck Reflex (STNR): this reflex usually integrates at 9-12 months. It supports the development of crawling, pulling to standing position and walking.

Integrated: when the reflex has served its purpose in supporting an area of development.

Core strength: the ability to use tummy and back muscles in a balanced way.

Gross motor skills: the use of large muscle groups such as those in the arms, legs and core to support a range of physical activities including crawling, rolling, pulling up and walking.

Early Years Outcomes

Passes toys from one hand to the other. Holds an object in each hand and brings them together in the middle e.g. holds two blocks and bangs them together.

Picks up small objects between thumb and fingers.

Holds pen or crayon using a whole hand (palmar) grasp and makes random marks with different strokes.

Enjoys the sensory experience of making marks in damp sand, paste or paint.

Links to the Characteristics of Effective Learning

PLAYING AND EXPLORING

Finding out and exploring

★ showing curiosity about objects, events and people

★ using senses to explore the world around them

★ engaging in open-ended activity

★ showing particular interests

e.g. the child participates eagerly in new experiences such as painting their hands for printing or mark making in gloop or mud.

CREATING AND THINKING CRITICALLY

Having their own ideas

★ finding new ways to do things

Making links

★ making links and noticing patterns in their experience

e.g. a practitioner notices that a child who has been exploring mark making with paint later makes the same marks in the damp sand. They support the child to make links in their learning by drawing the child's attention to the marks and talking about their earlier experiences (showing the child if an appropriate representation is available).

ACTIVE LEARNING

Being involved and concentrating

★ showing high levels of energy, fascination

★ paying attention to details

Keeping on trying

★ persisting with an activity when challenges occur

★ bouncing back after difficulties

e.g. even though it may be difficult, the child persists and pays close attention whilst using a plant spray to squirt water patterns outside.

SENSORY EXPERIENCES PALMAR GRASP PICKS UP OBJECTS HOLDS OBJECTS

Observation
What you may notice...

Assessment
What it may signify...

Observation	Assessment
Can the child pass toys from one hand to the other?	The child's awareness of their physical **mid line** is developing.
Can the child pick up small objects using fingers and thumb using their **pincer grip**?	The child is developing their **fine motor skills**.
Can the child hold a pencil or crayon in a **palmar** grasp?	The child's **fine motor skills** are developing in line with their **palmar reflex**.
Does the child make random marks using different strokes?	The child is developing an interest in mark making.
Does the child actively seek to participate in sensory activities?	The child is developing an interest in exploring their environment using their sense of touch.
	The child avoids exploring sensory experiences that involve certain textures or getting their hands dirty or covered.

By 12 months most children are developing a mature pincer grip and able to pick up small items.

Planning
What you can do...

This links to sections 7, 8, 9, and 10 of the Progress Checklist on p33.

Ensure available toys are easy to grip for small hands including some that make sounds when touched to encourage passing from hand to hand.

Provide opportunities for fun activities for using tongs, tweezers, connected chopsticks, plant spray bottles, turkey basters and squirty toys to develop the squeezing action needed to pick up small objects.

Provide a range of brightly coloured mark making items. Ensure there is a selection of sizes available, from chunky to adult, and that pencils are sharpened and felt tips all work.

Model initial mark making through pressing, patting and making lines and swirls.

Offer regular experiences for children to experience a range of dry and wet textures e.g. dry and wet sand, damp compost, cold custard, uncooked rice or dry lentils.

For children that may not be comfortable getting their hands covered in paint, **gloop** or other textures place the material inside a zip-lock bag to allow them to feel and manipulate without actually touching it.

Additional activities

These are additional activities to further support this stage of development.

Wind the bobbin

Sit the child on your knee with their back to you. Move their hands in time to the song, rolling their hands for winding the bobbin, bringing their hands together then apart for pull, pull, and then clapping their hands together for clap, clap, clap.

Pass the parcel

Play pass the parcel games with a small group. Ensure the parcel is wrapped loosely without too much sticky tape so that it comes off fairly easily. Play the music for short periods of time and make sure each child has plenty of turns.

Sensory fun

To increase the range of sensory experiences, encourage exploration of cooked and uncooked pasta, jelly, milk whip, yogurt, flour and cornflour (add water and sculpt), plasticine and modelling clay.

Disco dough

Press patterns in a lump of dough in time to the music using all **digit**s (separately and in combinations).

Finger isolation

Tell stories using finger puppets. Play finger football. Provide a range of keypad gadgets such as tills, calculators and phones, and finger paint brushes to strengthen fingers and develop **fine motor** skills.

Glossary of terms

Mid line: a medial line, especially the medial line or plane of the body.

Palmar grip: using the whole hand to hold onto and use objects.

Pincer grip: grasping an object between the thumb and forefinger. The ability to perform this task is a milestone of fine motor development in infants, usually occurring from 9 to 12 months of age.

Fine motor: movements that require a high degree of control and precision. These may include drawing, writing, cutting with scissors, using cutlery.

Palmar reflex: a primitive reflex that curls the fingers when the palm of the hand is tickled, also known as the 'grasp' reflex. This reflex exercises the hand muscles and supports fine motor control.

Gloop: cornflour and water mixed to varying consistencies.

Digit: a human finger or toe.

Name ....

Date						
Age in months						

Use different coloured pens to track assessments so that progress can be seen.
Tick 'yes' if the child is fully able to perform the movement.
Tick 'some difficulty' if the child can sometimes perform the movement but not easily.
Tick 'severe difficulty' if the child rarely or never performs the movement.

		Yes	Some difficulty	Severe difficulty
1a	Able to sit unsupported for 1 minute.			
1b	Able to sit unsupported, without anxiety, for longer than 1 minute.			
2a	When sitting, able to lean forward and grasp small objects without collapsing or falling over.			
2b	When sitting, unsupported, chooses to lean to left side to grasp small objects without falling over.			
2c	When sitting, unsupported, chooses to lean to right side to grasp small objects without falling over.			
3a	Able to use stable objects to pull to standing.			
3b	Chooses to frequently use stable objects to pull up to standing.			
4a	Able to use rolling as a means of travel to change location.			
4b	Able to use shuffling as a means of travel to change location.			
4c	Able to use crawling as a means of travel to change location.			
5a	Able to use stable objects to cruise round a room.			
5b	Able to walk with one or both hands held by an adult.			
6a	Able to take first steps when encouraged by an adult.			
6b	Confident to take first steps without adult support.			
7a	Able to pass an object from one hand to the other.			
8a	Able to pick up small objects using pincer grip.			
9a	Able to hold mark making implement in palmar grasp, using different strokes to make random marks.			
10a	Willing to participate in sensory activities.			

Time to Move © Karen Murphy and Trudi Fitzhenry, published by Featherstone 2014

8 – 20 months

Progress Checklist

16 – 26 months

Early Years Outcomes

Walks upstairs holding hand of adult.

Comes downstairs backwards on knees (crawling).

Begins to balance blocks to build a small tower.

Makes connections between their movement and the marks they make.

Links to the Characteristics of Effective Learning

PLAYING AND EXPLORING

Finding out and exploring

★ showing curiosity about objects, events and people

★ using senses to explore the world around them

★ engaging in open-ended activity

★ showing particular interests

Being willing to 'have a go'

★ seeking challenge

★ showing a 'can do' attitude

★ taking a risk, engaging in new experiences, and learning by trial and error

e.g. the child's exploratory drive prompts them to attempt to climb up steps and stable equipment even though they may not have fully mastered the skill of getting down. It is important that practitioners judge carefully when to support and when to encourage independence.

ACTIVE LEARNING

Being involved and concentrating

★ maintaining focus on their activity for a period of time

★ paying attention to details

Keeping on trying

★ persisting with activity when challenges occur

★ bouncing back after difficulties

Enjoying achieving what they set out to do

★ showing satisfaction in meeting their own goals

e.g. the child spends a long time playing with a shape-sorter using trial and error to correctly post the objects and delighting in their own success.

CREATING AND THINKING CRITICALLY

Having their own ideas

★ finding new ways to do things

Making links

★ making links and noticing patterns in their experience

★ developing ideas of grouping, sequences, cause and effect

Choosing ways to do things

★ planning, making decisions about how to approach a task

★ changing strategy as needed

e.g. while playing with the shape-sorter, the child is making mental links, noticing what has worked, and becoming aware of cause and effect. Practitioners can help the child to put their thoughts into words.

UPSTAIRS

DOWNSTAIRS

BUILDING

MARK MAKING

Observation
What you may notice...

Assessment
What it may signify...

Does the child put their arms up to be carried upstairs or seem reluctant to walk upstairs even with adult support?

The child may lack confidence, **core stability** or be fearful of falling.

Does the child walk upstairs holding an adult's hand?

The child is confident to try new activities and feels supported by adults.

Can the child crawl backwards downstairs on their knees?

The child is confident to explore independently and feels stable in the crawling position.

Does the child explore their environment freely, crawling over objects forwards and backwards?

The child is developing their **visual perception** and **spatial awareness** alongside balance and coordination.

Can the child balance objects, such as blocks, to make a small tower?

The child is developing their **fine motor** skills and their **visual perception** and **spatial awareness** relations.

Does the child show an interest in stacking as a **schema**?

The child is exploring a new-found skill through repeating an action or series of actions in order to further their understanding of their world.

Does the child make connections between their actions and the effect made on paper, in dough, sand or other materials?

The child is beginning to develop an understanding of cause and effect.

Planning
What you can do...

This links to sections 1, 2, 3, and 4 of the Progress Checklist on p39.

To develop initial confidence and a feeling of achievement, hold both hands when starting to climb steps or stairs. Gradually progress to holding one hand and guiding the child to hold the rail (if available) with the other.

Start by practising on steps with only two or three rises, increasing to greater numbers as confidence grows.

13 - 22 months: most children walk upstairs holding an adult's hand.

Provide a range of stable and safe objects both indoors and outdoors to practise going up and down e.g. low ladders attached to a small slide or climbing frame, soft play blocks.

Play games that involve opportunities to develop **core stability** through rocking, rolling and crawling e.g. set up a mini obstacle course where children crawl through tunnels, over a low stable object such as a large tyre, then into a cone shaped spinning seat where an adult spins them gently.

Continue to develop these skills by encouraging the child to build taller towers. If the blocks are suitable can they build a tower as tall as they are?

Provide a wide range of objects for the child to extend or develop their interest in stacking or building. Offer some that stack easily and some that need more careful positioning, such as cups designed for stacking or cups from plastic tea sets.

Most children are able to build a tower. 2 blocks: 11-18 months. 3 blocks: 18 months. 6+ blocks: 24 months

Continue to encourage and praise all efforts at initial mark making. Use **commentating** to establish or confirm an awareness of cause and effect e.g. *'Look at how you've made a hole in the dough with your finger! Well done!'*

Most children are crawling backwards down stairs or steps by 18 months.

Additional activities

These are additional activities to further support this stage of development.

Stretching cats

Child rests on their knees on all fours, pretending to be a waking cat. They lower their head to lap some milk, then stretch forward, lifting their head upwards and sit back on their heels whilst stretching out their paws and yawning. Repeat to slow music.

Counting cats

After playing 'stretching cats', the children add a rocking movement forwards and backwards whilst lapping their milk. Pick a number between one and five and the children have that many drinks of milk before sitting back on their heels and stretching.

Row, rock and roll your boat

Sing and act out this rhyme. If the child lacks stability or range of movement assist them by sitting them on your lap and holding onto them while you row, rock and roll the boat.

Stacking crates

Encourage counting on fingers, touching and unrolling each **digit** for each number.

Schema time

Be aware of any potential **schema**s that individuals or groups of children seem to engage in and plan to extend this by ensuring the environment is set up for children to follow their ideas. E.g. if a child seems to be very interested in **enclosing**, why not support them by making dens using blankets and large pegs to clip material onto stable furniture indoors and outside?

Glossary of terms

Core stability: the muscle group (including abdominals)responsible for stabilising the body and supporting posture.

Fine motor: movements that require a high degree of control and precision. These may include drawing, writing, cutting with scissors, using cutlery.

Visual perception: interpreting the surrounding environment using eye sight.

Spatial awareness: the recognition of the distance between objects and the ability to judg where you are in relation to objects.

Visual spatial relations: ability to recognize a shape, object, or letter when presented in different positions, for example, puzzles, block designs.

Schema: a repeated pattern of behaviour which supports a child in their exploration and understanding of their world. These may include **grasping**, **positioning**, **transporting**, and **enclosing**.

Commentating: speaking out loud about what you notice the child doing whilst you play alongside them. This provides them with new vocabulary and models correct speech.

Grasping: the child explores handling a range of objects in different sensory situations (e.g. slippery, dry, cold, warm).

Positioning: the child explores putting objects in particular positions (e.g. in lines, behind or under things).

Transporting: the child explores moving objects from one place to another, sometimes using a basket, wheelbarrow or pushchair.

Enclosing: the child explores building 3D enclosures using blocks or bricks or creates 2D border by putting lines around their paintings or drawings.

Digit: a human finger or toe.

Name ....

Date						
Age in months						

Use different coloured pens to track assessments so that progress can be seen.

Tick 'yes' if the child is fully able to perform the movement.

Tick 'some difficulty' if the child can sometimes perform the movement but not easily.

Tick 'severe difficulty' if the child rarely or never performs the movement.

		Yes	Some difficulty	Severe difficulty
1a	Does the child seek to be carried up stairs or steps?			
1b	Can the child walk up stairs or steps holding an adult's hand?			
2a	Can the child crawl backwards down stairs or steps on their knees?			
2b	Does the child explore a range of environments by crawling?			
3a	Can the child build a small tower? (Note number of objects stacked).			
3b	Does the child appear to be following a schema or specific interest? (Note schema or interest).			
4a	Does the child appear to connect the movement of their fingers or hands to what they produce on paper or in other materials?			

Time to Move © Karen Murphy and Trudi Fitzhenry, published by Featherstone 2014

TIME TO MOV

22 – 36 months

arly Years Outcomes

Runs safely on whole foot.

Walks upstairs or downstairs holding onto a rail, two feet to a step.

inks to the Characteristics of Effective Learning

PLAYING AND EXPLORING

Finding out and exploring

★ using senses to explore the world around them

★ engaging in open-ended activity

Being willing to 'have a go'

★ seeking challenge

★ showing a 'can do' attitude

★ taking a risk, engaging in new experiences, learning by trial and error

e.g. the child spends time going up and down stairs or steps, gradually going higher and with greater confidence. Practitioners should be on hand to encourage and support as necessary.

ACTIVE LEARNING

Being involved and concentrating

★ showing high levels of energy, fascination

Keeping on trying

★ persisting with an activity when challenges occur

Enjoying achieving what they set out to do

★ showing satisfaction in meeting their own goals

e.g. the child participates in running activities outside with practitioners. They may stumble, or trip but recover quickly and continue with the game. Practitioners need to use their professional judgement to decide the pace of the game and that the space available is safe.

CREATING AND THINKING CRITICALLY

Having their own ideas

★ finding new ways to do things

e.g. as the child becomes more stable they experiment with speed and direction when running.

Most children are able to run safely by 30 months.

22 – 36 months

UPSTAIRS

DOWNSTAIRS

Observation
What you may notice...

Does the child move through the whole foot when walking i.e. heel first then toe?

Can the child move through the whole foot when running?

Can the child walk upstairs or steps holding on to a rail, two feet to a step?

Does the child walk downstairs or steps, holding on to a rail, two feet to a step?

Assessment
What it may signify...

The child's **plantar** or **babinski primitive reflexes** are becoming integrated, enabling a natural walking movement or **gait**.

The child's balance and coordination are developing alongside their **visual perception** and **spatial awareness**.

The child is growing in confidence when tackling changes in height linked to **visual perception**. Their **gross motor** leg muscles are gaining strength.

The child is showing readiness for greater challenge in climbing and descending slopes and steps.

Planning
What you can do...

This links to sections 1 and 2 of the Progress Checklist on p53.

Encourage exploration of different surfaces with bare feet – grass, smooth pebbles, sand and paint; practise walking on toes and heels/raise awareness of toes and heels.

Blow bubbles outside for the child to chase and pop. This may support the development of a safe running movement.

Activities involving rising and falling on tip toes, climbing and crawling up and down an incline and exploration of the space around them.

Provide opportunities to practise going up and down small blocks of steps or soft play equipment independently. Encourage children to look at each step as they go downstairs rather than look out into the open space.

By 30 months most children are able to walk confidently up or down steps holding a rail.

Additional activities

These are additional activities to further support this stage of development.

The Grand Old Duke of York

Encourage children to stretch onto tip-toes during the 'up', squat and touch the floor during the 'down', and stand with a secure base, both feet planted firmly on the ground during the 'half-way up/down'.

Elastic work

Play *Tug of War* games, ensuring a balance of strength and adult participation for safety. Try *Follow My Leader* — using arms and legs to move the elastic, adults initiate the movements, children can be encouraged to take the lead when ready.

Brendan O'Hara

The 'Walking Song'. Taken from *Wally Wombat and his Mates* book and CD. This song encourages children to explore moving on their toes, heels and sides of their feet.

Eye tracing to support visual development

Move a finger puppet up and down slowly to encourage child to follow it with their eyes. If this is difficult for them, keep the puppet still whilst the child looks at it and nods their head. This supports the development of visual perception linked to depth when going downstairs.

Hop little bunnies

Sing the nursery rhyme with the children as they curl up on the floor. When it gets to the chorus, encourage bouncy bunny hops, using the leg muscles to **propel** the body upwards.

Glossary of terms

Plantar reflex: a primitive reflex which occurs after the pads beneath the toes on the sole of the foot have been firmly pressed. In children above 2 years of age and adults, the toes curve down and inwards — this is a healthy response.

Babinski reflex: a primitive reflex which occurs after the sole of the foot has been firmly stroked up the outside edge of the sole and along the pads beneath the toes. The big toe then moves upward or toward the top surface of the foot. The other toes fan out.

This reflex is normal in children up to 2 years old. It disappears as the child gets older.

Gait: a technical term for walking.

Visual perception: interpreting the surrounding environment using eye sight.

Spatial awareness: recognition of the distance between objects and the ability to judge where you are in relation to objects.

Gross motor: larger movements of arms, legs, feet, or the entire body (crawling, running, rolling, pulling up and jumping).

Propel: to cause to move forwards or onwards.

Early Years Outcomes

Squats with steadiness to rest or play with object on the ground, and rises to feet without using hands.

Climbs confidently and is beginning to pull themselves up on nursery play climbing equipment.

Can kick a large ball.

Links to the Characteristics of Effective Learning

PLAYING AND EXPLORING

Finding out and exploring

★ showing curiosity about objects, events and people

★ engaging in open-ended activity

Being willing to 'have a go'

★ initiating activities

★ seeking challenge

★ showing a 'can do' attitude

★ taking a risk, engaging in new experiences, and learning by trial and error

e.g. the child is eager to explore climbing equipment. Practitioners need to support the child to take risks and challenge themselves whilst keeping the child safe.

ACTIVE LEARNING

Being involved and concentrating

★ maintaining focus on their activity for a period of time

★ showing high levels of energy, fascination

Keeping on trying

★ persisting with activity when challenges occur

★ showing a belief that more effort or a different approach will pay off

★ bouncing back after difficulties

Enjoying achieving what they set out to do

★ enjoying meeting challenges for their own sake, rather than external rewards or praise

e.g. the child experiments repeatedly with ways of getting on and off, up and down or along the climbing equipment. They show clear delight when their efforts are successful.

CREATING AND THINKING CRITICALLY

Having their own ideas

★ finding ways to solve problems

★ finding new ways to do things

Making links

★ making links and noticing patterns in their experience

e.g. when walking on tip toes the child experiments with holding on to a friend for balance before attempting this by themselves.

22 – 36 months

SQUATS

CLIMBS

KICKS

Observation
What you may notice...

Does the child sit rather than squat when playing with an object on the floor?

Can the child squat steadily and play for a short time?

Can the child rise to their feet without using their hands?

Does the child choose to climb on available equipment?

Is the child able to use their arms to pull themself up on low-level climbing equipment?

Does the child wobble or fall when trying to kick a large ball?

Does the child remain stable when kicking a large ball?

Assessment
What it may signify...

The child has not yet developed secure **hip rotation** and **hip flexion** or has unsteady balance.

The child is developing good **hip rotation** and **hip flexion** and balance.

The child has good **gross motor** strength in their legs and good balance.

The child is developing the confidence and **core strength** needed to climb.

The child is developing their upper body strength and may be ready for further challenge when climbing.

The child may lack the ability to balance when standing on one foot.

The child has good balance when standing on one foot and may be ready to kick smaller balls.

Most children are able to kick a large ball by 30 months.

Planning
What you can do...

This links to sections 3, 4 and 5 of the Progress Checklist on p53.

Movement songs that encourage hip and leg movement, for example *Hokey Cokey*. Focus on the leg movements and add side to side movements to the song.

Provide opportunities for children to walk and balance on different flat surfaces including mats, carpet squares, gravel, pebbles and sand.

Activities involving climbing to a low level with adult support e.g. climbing on to a small stool to sit for snack.

Encourage children to explore large equipment by scrambling, climbing, swinging and reaching e.g. monkey bars, climbing nets, ladders.

Provide opportunities to walk into, then kick, large, light objects like balloons and blow up beach balls.

Provide a range of smaller balls of differing weights to kick.

Additional activities

These are additional activities to further support this stage of development.

Frogs and princes/princesses

Tell the children a magic spell has turned them into frogs. They hop around until you tinkle the tambourine to break the spell, when they can move like galloping princes or dancing princesses.

Row your boat

Encourage children to experiment with different sitting positions (remember to include significant details in any observations), and rock forwards and backwards as far as they are comfortable. In pairs, sit with legs outstretched in a 'V' position, feet touching, knees bent if necessary. Join hands to rock each other, gradually straightening legs and increasing the stretch.

Jack in the box games

Encourage curling up small on the ground and opening up wide quickly. Progress into squatting then jumping up.

Dingle dangle scarecrow

Encourage the children to join in with the song by jumping up and squatting or lying down.

Stepping stones

Provide simple stepping stones and balance equipment for children to explore.

Spinning games

Play spinning games using curved spinning seats like Bilibos or roundabouts.

Ball skills

Encourage the child to move whilst kicking or dribbling a larger ball. Take it in turns to aim the ball at a large target.

Glossary of terms

Hip flexion: when the hip moves the limb forwards towards the front of the body.

Hip rotation: when the hip turns the limb inwards or outwards.

Gross motor: larger movements of arms, legs feet, or the entire body (crawling, running, rolling pulling up and jumping).

Core strength: ability to use tummy and back muscles in a balanced way.

Early Years Outcomes

Turns pages in a book, sometimes several at once.

Shows control in holding and using jugs to pour, hammers, books and mark-making tools.

Beginning to use three fingers (tripod grip) to hold writing tools.

Imitates drawing simple shapes such as circles and lines.

May be beginning to show preference for dominant hand.

Links to the Characteristics of Effective Learning

PLAYING AND EXPLORING

Finding out and exploring

★ showing curiosity about objects, events and people

★ using senses to explore the world around them

★ engaging in open-ended activity

★ showing particular interests

Being willing to 'have a go'

★ initiating activities

★ seeking challenge

★ showing a 'can do' attitude

★ taking a risk, engaging in new experiences, and learning by trial and error

e.g. the child is often found in the book corner looking at books. They may have particular favourites that have been read to them on many occasions or enjoy looking for pictures of things that interest them.

ACTIVE LEARNING

Being involved and concentrating

★ maintaining focus on their activity for a period of time

★ showing high levels of energy, fascination

★ paying attention to details

Keeping on trying

★ persisting with activity when challenges occur

Enjoying achieving what they set out to do

★ showing satisfaction in meeting their own goals

★ enjoying meeting challenges for their own sake, rather than external rewards or praise

e.g. at snack time the child persists with their efforts to pour their chosen drink even though spillages occur.

TURNS PAGES

CONTROL

TRIPOD GRIP

DRAWING

DOMINANCE

Observation
What you may notice...

Assessment
What it may signify...

Can the child turn the pages of a book, often several at once?

The child is beginning to explore how books work and developing some control over page turning (increased **pincer grip**).

Does the child show control in holding and using jugs to pour, hammers, books and mark-making tools?

The child is beginning to explore tools and objects that require **hand-eye coordination** and **fine motor** skills. Their ability to hold, grasp and grip a range of objects is developing.

Does the child use three fingers (**tripod grip**) to hold a range of writing tools?

The child is beginning to develop their **tripod grip** (chunkier tools make this easier). The child's **fine motor** control is developing.

Does the child imitate drawing simple shapes such as circles and lines?

The child's awareness of mark making is developing alongside improved **fine motor** control.

Does the child show a preference for using their left or right hand?

The child may be forming a preference for a dominant hand. This enables the skill and strength of one hand to develop, for more accurate **fine motor** skills.

By 30 months most children enjoy familiar story books

Planning
What you can do...

This links to sections 6, 7, 8, 9 and 10 of the Progress Checklist on p53.

Model page-turning through sharing books and allowing the child to help you turn pages. Provide board books and fabric books with chunky pages that are easier to grasp and turn.

Place jugs, play tea sets and different containers in the water tray to encourage grasping, lifting and pouring.

Have tongs or plastic tweezers and a range of objects in the sand, water or investigation areas for children to pick up and sort.

Use pavement chalk to draw repeated circular shapes on the ground outside. Use a different colour in each hand and encourage large arm movements.

Allow the child to scrunch up old newspaper or tissue paper for a collage to build hand strength. Notice which hand they prefer, if any.

By 36 months most children are able to hold a pencil using a tripod grip.

By 30 months many are beginning to demonstrate hand dominance.

Additional activities

These are additional activities to further support this stage of development.

Lift the flap

Explore lift-the-flap books to further develop fine motor control.

Storage fun!

Pull the lids off empty tubs and packages and fill with small items. Replace the lids and children can shake to make a sound.

Workshop

Leave a range of safe tools in the construction area such as toy hammers, pliers, screwdrivers. These encourage a firm grip during play.

Mark making materials

Have a range of mark making equipment available in each area of the setting. Include chubby crayons, triangular pencils, gel pens, felt tips, chalk and squeezy glitter tubes. Provide triangular pencil grips and writing tools when encouraging early mark making. Make sure the materials are well-presented and in good condition.

Wash day

Encourage children to play with sponges in the water tray and squeeze them to fill containers or use to wash toys from the setting.

Threading and weaving

Provide opportunities for children to thread and weave a wide range of materials. Try threading chunky buttons and beads onto laces or wool and ribbon through and around cardboard templates. Use thick florist's ribbon on outside railings or fencing.

Sorting natural objects

Set up a sorting activity using dried beans, small shells or pebbles, and encourage the use of **pincer grip** to pick up each item.

Musical clackers

Support children in playing with castanets, using thumb and two fingers to push the castanet sides together.

Bang a beat

Work with the child to bang out a pulse on a drum or wooden block, using a beater. Encourage accurate and firm rhythm. Extend by using a coloured xylophone – can the child hit each coloured note individually?

If I had a hammer…

Make wooden pegs and hammer sets available. Encourage the child to hammer the pegs in through the holes.

Snow spray art

Fill plant sprayers with coloured water (use food colouring) and allow the child to create large works of art in the snow.

Glossary of terms

Pincer grip: grasping an object between the thumb and forefinger. The ability to perform this task is a milestone of fine motor development in infants, usually occurring from 9 to 12 months of age.

Hand-eye coordination: ability to use the eyes and hands together to perform an activity, for example, stringing beads, completing puzzles, playing board games.

Fine motor: movements that require a high degree of control and precision. These may include drawing, writing, cutting with scissors, using cutlery.

Visual spatial relations: ability to recognize a shape, object, or letter when presented in different positions, for example, puzzles, block designs.

Tripod grip (on objects): thumb, index, and middle fingers; less mature than pincer grasp; tripod grasp (on writing implement): three fingers, thumb, index, and middle fingers.

Progress Checklist: 22 – 36 months

Name ....

Date						
Age in months						

Use different coloured pens to track assessments so that progress can be seen.

Tick 'yes' if the child is fully able to perform the movement.

Tick 'some difficulty' if the child can sometimes perform the movement but not easily.

Tick 'severe difficulty' if the child rarely or never performs the movement.

		Yes	Some difficulty	Severe difficulty
1a	The child is able to move through the whole foot when walking, placing the heel down first followed by the toes.			
1b	The child is able to move through the whole foot when running.			
2a	The child is able to walk upstairs or steps holding on to a rail, two feet to a step.			
2b	The child is able to walk downstairs or steps, holding on to a rail, two feet to a step.			
3a	The child is able to squat steadily for a few minutes whilst playing.			
3b	The child is able to rise to their feet from squatting without using their hands.			
4a	The child climbs low-level equipment.			
4b	The child uses their arms to pull themselves up on to low-level climbing equipment.			
5a	The child can kick a large ball whilst remaining stable.			
6a	The child is able to turn pages in a book – note how many at a time.			
7a	The child shows some control when holding and using a range of tools and equipment.			
8a	The child can demonstrate a tripod grip when holding a slim mark making tool.			
9a	The child is able to draw simple shapes when this is modelled by a practitioner.			
10a	The child is beginning to show a preference for a dominant hand – note which hand.			

Time to Move © Karen Murphy and Trudi Fitzhenny, published by Featherstone 2014

Early Years Outcomes

Moves freely and with pleasure and confidence in a range of ways, such as: slithering, shuffling and rolling.

Moves freely and with pleasure and confidence in a range of ways, such as: crawling, walking and running.

Moves freely and with pleasure and confidence in a range of ways, such as: jumping, skipping, sliding and hopping.

Links to the Characteristics of Effective Learning

PLAYING AND EXPLORING

Being willing to 'have a go'

* initiating activities

* seeking challenge

* showing a 'can do' attitude

* taking a risk, engaging in new experiences, and learning by trial and error

e.g. the child will begin to explore smooth surfaces with their feet, slithering and shuffling them across the floor. The practitioner can extend the challenge by suggesting sliding and slithering using different body parts e.g on the back or tummy.

ACTIVE LEARNING

Enjoying achieving what they set out to do

* showing satisfaction in meeting their own goals

* being proud of how they accomplished something – not just the end result

* enjoying meeting challenges for their own sake rather than external rewards or praise

e.g. the child shows an interest in hopping. They try to hop on alternate feet and achieve this when holding on to the practitioner's hand. They are excited to share their achievement, wanting to be seen in the act of hopping. It is important that the practitioner praises the child's efforts and how they managed to hop by themselves, not just the ability to hop.

CREATING AND THINKING CRITICALLY

Having their own ideas

* thinking of ideas

* finding ways to solve problems

* finding new ways to do things

e.g. the child is role playing a rainforest and decides they will be a monkey. They move over, under and around equipment by swinging their bodies and climbing from space to space. The practitioner can develop the activity by introducing new equipment to move along, encouraging the child's monkey-like movements across high and low spaces.

SLITHERING, SHUFFLING, ROLLING

CRAWLING, WALKING, RUNNING

JUMPING, SKIPPING, SLIDING, HOPPING

Observation
What you may notice…

Is the child reluctant to move on their tummy when slithering?

Can the child shuffle on their bottom using their arms and legs to move themselves forwards or backwards?

Can the child shuffle on their bottom without using their arms?

Can the child roll from side to side when lying down without using their hands (sausage roll)?

Can the child crawl on all fours, forwards and backwards?

Can the child walk with a normal heel to toe gait?

Does the child run freely, with pleasure and confidence?

Can the child jump from two feet to land on two feet on a flat surface, using bent knees to **w** themselves?

Can the child skip on the spot?

Can the child skip whilst moving forwards?

Can the child slide on their feet? On their bottom?

Does the child hop?

Assessment
What it may signify…

The child may feel discomfort due to poor bladder control.

The child is developing the use of their **gross motor** skills.

The child is developing **core strength**.

The child is demonstrating good muscle control.

The child is demonstrating physical control and coordination.

The child is demonstrating the ability to move forwards in a coordinated fashion.

The child is demonstrating the ability to **propel** themselves forward with both feet leaving the ground.

The child is demonstrating the confidence to leave the ground unaided.

The child is able shift their weight from one foot to the other, in a coordinated hopping movement.

The child is developing the ability to **propel** themselves forwards whilst skipping.

The child is developing their **proprioceptive feedback** through exploring pushing their feet or bodies in a sliding movement.

The child is developing the balance and coordination to leave the ground unaided and land safely.

Planning
What you can do...

This links to section 1 of the Progress Checklist on p67.

Provide opportunities for the child to lie on their tummy when playing e.g. with train sets.

Sing action songs that involve shuffling forwards and backwards such as Brendan O'Hara's *Spin on your bottom*.

Sing *Row, row, row your boat,* keeping the arms in the air and pulling them towards the body as the legs help to row (shuffle) forwards in the imaginary boat.

Wrap the child in a blanket or large piece of lycra material and gently pull to unroll it. Allow space for the child to continue rolling.

Encourage the children to move to music and pretend to be a cat or another four legged animal e.g. *Everybody wants to be a cat* (Aristocats, Disney soundtrack).

Provide experiences for the children to identify and feel the different parts of their feet e.g. making toe and heel prints on paper.

Provide opportunities for racing and chasing games such as 'corners'. Place four different coloured cones, one in each corner, then instruct the children to run, skip, crawl, roll, hop, slither or slide to a specific colour.

Put on wellies and go outside to jump in puddles on a rainy day!

Start with marching on the spot to music, adding in a 'hop' (by encouraging the child to jump off one foot) to turn the movement into skipping. Gradually increase the hopping until it becomes a skip.

Stand in a circle with joined hands. Take turns to skip around each other whilst singing *In and out the dusty bluebells*. You can create arches with joined hands.

Take it in turns to sit on a large piece of lycra and pull each other along a smooth surface. Ensure the children are supervised and the area is safe.

Practise hopping into and out of a hoop or a spot on the floor.

Additional activities

These are additional activities to further support this stage of development.

Floor play

Provide a large whiteboard or roll of paper and pens on the floor to encourage children to lie on their tummies when mark making.

Jack and Jill

Encourage children to crawl up a low hill and roll down on their sides, singing the nursery rhyme. Make sure there are no obstacles in the way!

Tiggy on the floor

The children play a crawling-based game of tig, where they chase each other around a space crawling on all fours and freeze if they are caught. You can use mats to act as safe bases. Shake some sleigh bells to free all those who are 'stuck'. This can be adapted so the children roll around the space.

Commando movements

Allow children to practise different ways of crawling, sliding and slithering under a camouflage net or parachute. Extend this activity by adding an obstacle course that includes tunnels, steps and swinging ropes or bars (where possible).

Fire! Fire!

Chalk a ladder onto the ground outside and chalk a simple fire picture at the top. Place a bucket with water and a sponge at the bottom. Encourage the children to collect the sponge and hop to the top rung, then put the fire out with the sponge. Can extend challenge by hopping on the non-dominant foot.

Skip to my Lou

Sing this traditional rhyme whilst skipping round the room.

Squirrel nutkin

Place hoops on the ground as squirrel nests. Scatter beanbags in the spaces between. The children work in pairs to gather a certain coloured 'nut' one at a time and get back to their nest before the others. Can be played crawling or running.

Tightrope walking

Create a 'tightrope' on the floor using masking tape. Encourage the children to walk along the tightrope placing their heels down first, followed by their toes, using arms to balance. To increase the challenge, show the children how to bring their feet closer together so the feet almost touch heel to toe. Give them a drum roll as they walk along!

Glossary of terms

Gait: a technical term for walking.

Propel: to cause to move forwards or onwards

Gross motor skills: the use of large muscle groups such as those in the arms, legs and cor to support a range of physical activities includin crawling, rolling, pulling up and walking. They develop in infancy in a head to toe order.

Core strength: the ability to use tummy and back muscles in a balanced way.

Proprioceptive feedback: sensory feedbac that tells us where our body parts are in space without having to look e.g. being able to put an object into our mouth. It also helps us to know how much force we need to use to do somethi e.g. how hard to grip something without squashing it or how to throw a ball so that it go far enough but not too far. Activities involving resistance give us the most feedback.

Non-dominant: the arm/hand or leg/foot that the child does not usually choose to use for kicking a ball, handling tools etc.

Early Years Outcomes

Mounts stairs, steps or climbing equipment using alternate feet.

Walks downstairs, two feet to each step while carrying a small object.

Runs skilfully and negotiates space successfully, adjusting speed or direction to avoid obstacles.

Can stand momentarily on one foot when shown. Can catch a large ball.

Links to the Characteristics of Effective Learning

PLAYING AND EXPLORING

Being willing to 'have a go'

★ initiating activities

★ seeking challenge

★ showing a 'can do' attitude

★ taking a risk, engaging in new experiences, and learning by trial and error

e.g. the child wants to climb back down the steps of the slide and is initially reluctant. The practitioner can help them to feel where to put their feet to descend safely. The child climbs down independently then repeats the activity to test it out again.

CREATING AND THINKING CRITICALLY

Choosing ways to do things

★ planning, making decisions about how to approach a task, solve a problem and reach a goal

★ checking how well their activities are going

★ changing strategy as needed

★ reviewing how well the approach worked

e.g. the child is playing a cycling game involving moving in and around cones. The child tries to steer the tricycle between the cones and knocks one over. They move the cones further apart and try again. The practitioner can support learning by asking how this worked or by increasing challenge with the addition of new obstacles to cycle between.

ACTIVE LEARNING

Keeping on trying

★ persisting with activity when challenges occur

★ showing a belief that more effort or a different approach will pay off

★ bouncing back after difficulties

Enjoying achieving what they set out to do

★ enjoying meeting challenges for their own sake, rather than external rewards or praise

e.g. the child is playing a catching game with a medium-sized ball. When they miss the ball they try to stand nearer, to increase their chances of catching it. They continue to try different stances and different grasps until they successfully catch the ball. It is important that the practitioner allows the child to explore different strategies and offers verbal encouragement as they bounce the ball back.

STAISR AND STEPS

DOWNSTAIRS

RUNNING

CATCH A BALL
STAND ON ONE FOOT

Observation
What you may notice…

Can the child go up two or three steps using alternate feet whilst holding on to something?

Does the child mount stairs or steps using alternate feet?

Can the child climb small ladders on climbing equipment using alternate feet and hands?

Can the child walk down some steps unaided?

Can the child walk downstairs and carry a small object?

Does the child walk downstairs two feet at a time whilst carrying a small object?

Can the child run in an open space near other children without knocking into them?

Does the child run skilfully in and out of obstacles or other children?

Can the child change speed or direction when running to avoid obstacles and other children?

Can the child stand on one foot unaided when shown?

Can the child catch a large ball thrown at them with both hands/arms?

Assessment
What it may signify…

The child is beginning to explore balance and the coordination needed to climb low obstacles.

The child is developing balance and coordination skills.

The child's **upper** and **lower gross motor** muscles are working together to enable climbing.

The child is developing accurate **visual perception**.

The child is becoming more confident with their sense of balance.

The child is more secure in their **core stability** and can negotiate steps without needing arms to aid balance.

The child is developing their **spatial awareness**.

The child's **visual skills** and **motor skills** are developing to enable greater **spatial awareness**.

The child is able to respond to obstacles in their line of vision by adjusting their speed (speeding up or slowing down) or moving in a different direction.

The child's **core stability** is beginning to develop, leading to greater balance and control.

The child can react quickly to moving **visual stimuli**, enabling an accurate gross motor response.

Planning
What you can do...

This links to sections 2, 3, 4, 5 and 6 of the Progress Checklist on p67.

Make secure steps using large wooden blocks or beams and hold the child's hand as they explore stepping on and off these.

Provide a small slide with two or three steps for the child to practise going up whilst holding on to the rail.

Stand behind or near to the child as they attempt to climb a ladder on a climbing frame, increasing your distance as they become more confident.

Using secure crates or large rubber tyres, hold the child's hand as they jump off them. Repeat until the child is confident enough to step down rather than jump.

Play stair counting games, encouraging the child to step down and stand on each step, saying each number in sequence.

Create a simple bridge with steps at either side for the child to climb up and down. Encourage them to carry a basket or toy across to deliver to the other side.

Give the children coloured ribbons or streamers to run with, encouraging them to keep their ribbons away from the others.

Play simple running games involving dodging cones or hoops.

Make paper kites with short string and 'fly' it by running around outside and trailing it behind.

Allow the child to hold on to your hand as they stand on one leg, then the other.

Start by rolling a large, soft ball towards the child so they can learn how to react to its speed. Then throw it from a close distance into their arms.

At around 36 months many children are able to catch a large ball with both hands when thrown from a short distance.

Additional activities

These are additional activities to further support this stage of development.

Low ladder fun

Make a ladder on the floor using chalk or ropes so the child can step in and out of the rungs.

Climbing trees song

Encourage a cross-lateral movement by singing *I like climbing trees for apples* (Brendan O'Hara).

Explore climbing

Take the child to a park or play area where there are a variety of climbing surfaces to explore, including low climbing nets or climbing wall pegs. Ensure that risk assessments have been completed prior to the outing and that the child is well supervised at all times.

Obstacle course

Using available resources such as hoops, ropes, stepping stones and small sets of wooden steps or slides, create a simple obstacle course for children to negotiate their way around. Add challenge and develop problem solving by encouraging them to keep their feet off the ground.

One legged song

Play a short piece of music and see how long a child can stand on one leg before changing to the other. Encourage fun wobbling and use of arms to aid stability.

Animal hops

Create a simple story for the children to move to, including animals that hop like frogs, rabbits and kangaroos.

Imaginary chocolate game

Describe an item the child really likes e.g. chocolate and ask them to imagine you are throwing a large bar of it for them to catch and eat. Encourage the child to reach out and grab the object and pull it close to them. This helps teach the skill of catching.

Easy peesy game

Throw and ctach large, soft objects such as polystyrene-filled bean bags with ribboned tails, soft- bodied toys with arms and legs and large koosh balls that are easy to grasp.

Glossary of terms

Upper and lower gross motor muscles: t larger muscles in the arms and legs.

Visual perception: interpreting the surroundir environment using eye sight.

Core stability: the muscle group (including abdominals)responsible for stabilising the body and supporting posture.

Spatial awareness: the recognition of the distance between objects and the ability to judg where you are in relation to objects.

Visual skills: the ability to perceive what is see

Motor skills: relating to physical movement (se also gross and fine motor skills).

Visual stimuli: Something that provokes a response from the eyes e.g. a picture, toy, objec or person.

Gross motor: the larger movements of arms, legs, feet, or the entire body (crawling, running and jumping.

Horizontal: relating to the horizon, e.g. a line going for left to right.

arly Years Outcomes

Draws lines and circles using gross motor movements.

Uses one-handed tools and equipment, e.g. makes snips in paper with child scissors.

Holds pencil between thumb and two fingers, no longer using whole-hand grasp.
Holds pencil near point between first two fingers and thumb and uses it with good control.

Can copy some letters, e.g. letters from their name.

inks to the characteristics of effective learning

PLAYING AND EXPLORING

Being willing to 'have a go'

★ initiating activities

★ seeking challenge

★ showing a 'can do' attitude

★ taking a risk, engaging in new experiences, and learning by trial and error

e.g. the child takes a paintbrush and water pot and draws a long, wavy line on the ground. They repeat this pattern, saying they are drawing the sea to have a paddle in. The practitioner could introduce the letter 's' for 'sea' and show the child how it is like the wavy lines they have painted.

ACTIVE LEARNING

Being involved and concentrating

★ maintaining focus on their activity for a period of time

★ showing high levels of energy, fascination

★ not getting easily distracted

★ paying attention to details

e.g. the child is using a hole punch to create patterns in the paper. They press the handle carefully and move it around the edges of the paper, watching the holes appear with interest. The practitioner could introduce different patterned paper punches for the child to explore.

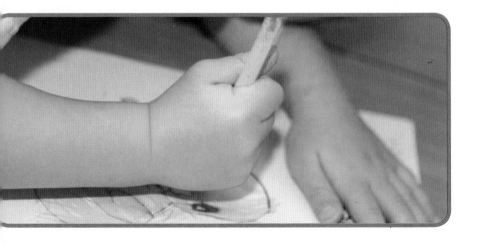

63

DRAWING LINES · ONE-HANDED TOOLS · PENCIL CONTROL · COPYING LETTERS

Observation What you may notice…		Assessment What it may signify…
Can the child create lines and circles using **gross motor** movements?	▷	The child is beginning to explore **gross motor** movements and upper body coordination.
Does the child choose to create and draw lines and circles using gross motor (large muscle) movements across a range of activities?	▷	The child is developing some control over upper body coordination and **gross motor** muscles.
Can the child use scissors and other one-handed tools and equipment?	▷	The child may be unsure of dominant hand or lack appropriate grip, elements of **palmar reflex** may be present.
Does the child choose to use scissors and other one-handed tools and equipment, with confidence?	▷	The child has established hand dominance and their grip is secure, their **hand-eye coordination** is developing.
Does the child use a whole hand or fist grip to hold a pencil or mark making tool?	▷	The child has not yet developed their **pincer grip** and their **gross motor** muscles are relied on for mark making.
Does the child use their first two fingers and thumb to hold pencils/tools near the point?	▷	The child's **pincer grip** and **fine motor** control skills are developing.
Can the child use a correct pencil grip with good control?	▷	The child is showing readiness for letter and number formation.
Can the child trace over letters e.g. letters from their name?	▷	The child's **fine motor** control is developing alongside their hand-eye coordination.
Can the child copy some letters e.g. letters from their name?	▷	The child is showing readiness for letter and number formation.

Planning
What you can do...

This links to sections 7, 8, 9 and 10 of the Progress Checklist on p67.

Encourage games involving ribbons on sticks or bubble wands to form circles and patterns in the air. Use both arms at the same time to develop **gross motor** awareness.

Provide large sheets of paper, interactive whiteboards or other **vertical** surfaces for painting, drawing and exploring lines and circles using full arm movements.

Play games that encourage development of strength in fingers and thumb. Pinching, squeezing and poking clay in time to music, using all **digit**s.

Play target games to develop hand-eye coordination e.g. bean bags in a bucket. This also encourages grasp and release of objects.

Explore pegs and peg boards or large Hama beads, making patterns and lines as the child learns how to pick up small objects using fingers and thumb. Progress to smaller objects to pick up and sort or small pieces of food to pick up and eat.

When **pincer grip** is established, offer different tracing activities to encourage pencil control. Draw around templates and stencils, then colour the pictures created. Complete maze puzzles tracing the route through with fingers then following with crayons.

Teach correct letter formation and provide a range of tools and textures to explore the shape of each letter.

Tactile and multi-sensory tracing activities e.g. following a route through the sand with your fingers or a toy car, drawing shapes in shaving foam or gloop, finger painting letters from your name.

Feely bag letters and numbers – identifying them through their shape. Tracing fingers along sandpaper letters and numbers. Painting letters in puddles or with water on the wall.

By 48 months most children are able to copy some basic letter shapes.

Additional activities

These are additional activities to further support this stage of development.

Doodling fun

Tape a large sheet of paper to a vertical surface and provide chalks, chunky pens, paintbrushes and finger paints for the children to use. Draw a **vertical** line down the centre of the paper and encourage the children to use a pen in each hand when drawing and doodling circles, lines and patterns. Progress to paper laid horizontally. Ensure the vertical line is in front of the child's physical mid-line.

Hand massage (for poor pencil grip)

Gently squeeze along each finger and thumb, front and back, side to side, holding at the tip.

Song time

Sing finger rhymes like *Tommy Thumb*, encouraging the child to isolate and move each digit in turn. Use finger puppets to bring the characters to life.

1,2,3,4,5

Encourage counting on fingers, touching and unrolling each **digit** for each number.

Squeeze me tight

Offer a **tactile** stress ball or other object to manipulate and squeeze – this will encourage the palmar reflex.

Musical fingers

Provide a weighted keyboard or piano – so children can press each key in turn using each finger to make a sound. This develops finger strength.

Collage

Encourage children to screw up tiny pieces of paper with their fingers and thumb to develop fine motor control. Glue them to a collage using fingers to spread the glue.

Worm rolling

Provide playdough for children to roll between hands, then between fingers to make worms or spaghetti.

Confetti fun

Encourage children to cut patterns and strips from scrap paper – make confetti by snipping different coloured sheets. Work towards cutting along a curved or zig zag line.

Baking fun

Make bread together and knead, pull, shape and twist the dough.

Glossary of terms

Gross motor: larger movements of arms, legs, feet, or the entire body (crawling, running and jumping).

Palmar reflex: a reflex that curls the fingers when the palm of the hand is tickled, also known as the 'grasp' reflex. This reflex exercises the hand muscles and supports fine motor control.

Pincer grip: grasping an object between the thumb and forefinger. The ability to perform this is a milestone of fine motor development in infancy usually occurring from 9 to 12 months of age.

Fine motor: movements that require a high degree of control and precision. These may include drawing, writing, cutting with scissors and using cutlery.

Vertical: a line in space going from top to bottom or bottom to top.

Digit: human finger or toe.

Tactile: affecting the sense of touch.

Hand-eye coordination: ability to use the hands and eyes together to perform an activity e.g. stringing beads, completing puzzles, playing board games.

Dominant hand: the hand a child regularly and instinctively uses for fine motor skills.

Name ....

Date						
Age in months						

Use different coloured pens to track assessments so that progress can be seen.
Tick 'yes' if the child is fully able to perform the movement.
Tick 'some difficulty' if the child can sometimes perform the movement but not easily.
Tick 'severe difficulty' if the child rarely or never performs the movement.

		Yes	Some difficulty	Severe difficulty
1a	Able to jump from two feet to land on two feet, using bent knees.			
1b	Able to skip on the spot.			
1c	Able to skip moving forwards.			
1d	Able to slide on their feet and bottom.			
1e	Able to hop (note which foot).			
2a	Able to climb 2 or 3 steps, holding on to something or someone.			
2b	Able to climb stairs or steps unaided with alternate feet.			
3a	Able to walk down stairs or steps unaided.			
3b	Able to walk down stairs or steps carrying a small object.			
4a	Able to run in an open space without collision.			
4b	Able to run in an open space and adjust speed or direction.			
5	Able to stand on one foot unaided when shown. Note how long for and which foot.			
6	Able to catch a large ball.			
7a	Able to create lines using gross motor movements (e.g. waving ribbons).			
7b	Able to create circles using gross motor movements (e.g. waving ribbons).			
8a	Able to hold and use scissors correctly to cut paper.			
8b	With one hand, able to use a press to squeeze shapes in dough.			
9a	Able to demonstrate a correct pencil grip			
9b	Able to apply appropriate pressure when using tools (e.g. Pencils, screwdrivers).			
10a	Able to trace over letters.			
10b	Able to copy some letters.			

Time to Move © Karen Murphy and Trudi Fitzhenry, published by Featherstone 2014

TIME TO M

40 – 60+ months

Early Years Outcomes

Experiments with different ways of moving.

Jumps off an object and lands appropriately.

Negotiates space successfully when playing racing and chasing games with other children, adjusting speed or changing direction to avoid obstacles.

Travelling with confidence and skill around, under, over and through balancing and climbing equipment.

Links to the Characteristics of Effective Learning

PLAYING AND EXPLORING

Finding out and exploring

★ using senses to explore the world around them

★ engaging in open-ended activity

Being willing to 'have a go'

★ seeking challenge

★ showing a 'can do' attitude

★ taking a risk, engaging in new experiences, learning by trial and error

e.g. the child will spend time exploring their environment and work with available resources to create bridges, paths, tunnels and dens. They will figure out how to balance objects securely and how to safely move over and under things through testing them out. It is important that practitioners support the child's creative exploration and work with the child to eliminate risks.

ACTIVE LEARNING

Being involved and concentrating

★ showing high levels of energy, fascination

Keeping on trying

★ persisting with activities when challenges occur

Enjoying achieving what they set out to do

★ showing satisfaction in meeting their own goals

e.g. the child spends extended periods of time creating their environment, finding new ways to do things when challenges occur and taking pride in their own achievements.

CREATING AND THINKING CRITICALLY

Having their own ideas

★ finding new ways to do things

e.g. the child will continue to work on their structures or obstacle courses with other children or alone, returning to the same activity until it is completed to their satisfaction. They will be willing to try different arrangements of objects or different ways of moving if their first attempts are unsuccessful. The practitioner can be on hand to join in the problem solving but not to direct it.

40 – 60+ months

DIFFERENT WAYS OF MOVING

JUMPING

NEGOTIATING SPACE

TRAVELLING WITH CONFIDENCE

Observation
What you may notice…

Can the child move in a range of different ways including travelling, balancing and moving to music?

Is the child able to jump off a raised object such as a gymnastics bench and land safely on both feet?

Can the child negotiate and share an open space with other children during a race or chasing game?

Is the child able to adjust their speed or change direction to avoid bumping into objects?

Does the child move confidently around objects, showing some skill in going under, over and through equipment on the floor such as hoops?

Can the child skilfully travel around, under, over and through balancing and climbing equipment such as mini obstacle courses?

Assessment
What it may signify…

The child is growing in confidence physically and can make choices about how they move their body.

The child has developed good **gross motor** coordination and balance.

The child is gaining a good sense of **spatial awareness**.

The child demonstrates increased **core stability** and **spatial awareness**.

Planning
What you can do...

This links to section 1, 2, 3 and 4 of the Progress Checklist on p86.

Provide a range of music for the children to listen to in a space where they can move around freely. If possible, provide tall mirrors so the children can watch themselves as they explore different patterns of movement.

Place large hoops around the floor in an open space. Play music or shake a tambourine as the children skip between them. When you bang the tambourine they have to jump and land in the nearest hoop. Encourage a correct landing technique – the legs should be slightly bent at the knees and the back should be straight. Remind the children to always land on the balls of their feet and not on flat feet.

Sing together a traditional rhyme like *In and out the dusty bluebells*. One child is chosen and stands aside while the others form a circle with their hands joined up in arches. The chosen child weaves in and out of the circle whilst everyone sings the rhyme. At the 'tippy tappy' part, the chosen child stands facing another child whilst everyone touches their opposite hand to knee. These children then form a train and weave in and out as the song begins again. Continue until the last child joins the train.

Create a set of physical challenges for the children to enjoy. Include low benches, tunnels, climbing frames, sheets of fabric – anything that the child can safely crawl over, under, through or along using different parts of their body.

Additional activities

These are additional activities to further support this stage of development.

Row your boat (in pairs)

Encourage children to experiment with different sitting positions (remember to include significant details in observations), and rock forwards and backwards as far as they are comfortable. In pairs, sit with legs outstretched in a 'V' position, feet touching, knees bent if necessary. Join hands to rock each other, gradually straightening legs and increasing the stretch.

Bean game

Encouraging awareness of space and direction, children respond to the bean called out e.g. runner bean – running in and out and around each other; frozen bean – stand still both feet firmly planted; jelly bean – shaking and wobbling all body parts then 'melting' into the floor; up the beanstalk – **homolateral** and **cross-lateral** climbing onto tip-toes. Add drum beat and rhythm to the running to support reading development.

Mr Men game

Similar to 'the bean game' but using Mr Men and Little Miss characters to inspire a range of movements. Mr Tall – stretch up high; Mr Small – squat down low; Mr Fast – run around; Little Miss Sunshine – sparkle arms out wide etc.

Hop little bunnies

Sing the song as the children lie, curled up on the floor. At the point of singing 'wake up little bunnies' show the children how to bunny-hop around the space, travelling from two feet to two feet.

Hopscotch

Chalk a hopscotch outside or place carpet squares in the shape of the hopscotch. Show the children how to move from one foot to two feet, then back to one as they hop through the squares. This game also develops the child's ability to jump from two feet to land on one.

Road race

Set up an outdoor obstacle course wide enough for children to access using bikes, scooters and trikes. Chalk a large roundabout at the end with arrows to aid safe directionality. Use low ramps, cones and traffic signs (if available). Demonstrate how to use the course and supervise this activity to ensure safety.

Mulberry bush

Sing the song with a group of children, changing the range of movements explored to link to your current topic or theme.

Glossary of terms

Gross motor: is the coordination and control of the large muscle groups and relate to whole body movement. They develop in infancy in a head to toe order.

Spatial awareness: the recognition of the distance between objects and the ability to judge where you are in relation to objects.

Core stability: the muscle group (including abdominals) responsible for stabilising the body and supporting posture.

Homolateral: a one sided movement—left hand and foot together then right hand and foot together.

Cross-lateral: a movement that crosses the mid line of the body—right hand and left foot together, left hand and right foot together.

Early Years Outcomes

Shows increasing control over an object in pushing, patting, throwing, catching or kicking it.

Uses simple tools to effect changes to materials.

Handles tools, objects, construction and malleable materials safely and with increasing control.

Links to the Characteristics of Effective Learning

PLAYING AND EXPLORING

Finding out and exploring

★ showing curiosity about objects, events and people

★ engaging in open-ended activity

★ showing particular interests

Playing with what they know

★ pretending objects are things from their experiences

Being willing to 'have a go'

★ taking a risk, engaging in new experiences, and learning by trial and error

e.g. the child will play with a range of available tools as part of their imaginative play. They will explore how everyday objects such as whisks, rollers, spoons and pizza wheels work when playing with dough, gloop or in a mud kitchen. The practitioner can model the correct use of everyday tools and can engage in pretend play with imaginary tools.

ACTIVE LEARNING

Being involved and concentrating

★ maintaining focus on their activity for a period of time

★ showing high levles of energy, fascination

★ not easily distracted

★ paying attention to details

Keeping on trying

★ persisting with activity when challenges occur

★ showing a belief that more effort or a different approach will pay off

★ bouncing back after difficulties

e.g. the child will continue to operate the pretend drill when building their house, focusing on this activity for an extended period of time. They may try different tools or techniques. It is important for the practitioner to encourage and praise the child when they continue to adapt their ideas to find a way that works.

CREATING AND THINKING CRITICALLY

Having their own ideas

★ thinking of ideas

★ finding new ways to do things

Making links

★ making predictions and testing their ideas

★ developing ideas of grouping, sequences, cause and effect

Choosing ways to do things

★ planning, making decisions about how to approach a task

★ checking how well their activities are going

★ changing strategy as needed

e.g. the child may work with others to create a structure. They will talk about their ideas and test them out, sorting the bricks they need into shapes or colours. The practitioner can help by asking questions about what the children are creating, what works well and what happens if their ideas don't work.

INCREASING CONTROL

USES TOOLS

HANDLES TOOLS

Observation
What you may notice...

Assessment
What it may signify...

Does the child show increasing control when throwing, catching or kicking?

▶ The child demonstrates more accurate **visual perception** and **spatial awareness** alongside balance and coordination and increased **core stability**.

Does the child demonstrate accuracy when pushing or patting objects?

▶ The child is developing strength and control over their upper body **gross motor** movements and **fine motor** skills.

Can the child use simple tools to produce self-chosen results?

▶ The child is developing greater understanding of cause and effect.

Can the child use tools and equipment safely?

▶ The child is beginning to understand some aspects of safe handling and make their own risk assessments.

Does the child use a range of tools and materials with increasing control?

▶ The child is developing their **fine motor** skills.

Planning
What you can do...

This links to section 5, 6 and 7 of the Progress Checklist on p86.

Play games that encourage throwing, catching and kicking e.g. hoops suspended at different heights with a range of different sized balls that can be thrown or kicked through the hoops. Play team games that include dribbling a ball round objects.

Provide resources that develop **manipulative skills** and require increased pressure or strength e.g. using clay or hard plasticine to mould and make objects.

Provide an interesting range of materials and appropriate tools to encourage children to experiment and discover ways of manipulating materials to produce new and different objects and patterns.

Continue to be vigilant around demonstrating the use of new or potentially dangerous equipment and encourage the child to assess risk for themselves though discussion e.g. prior to children starting free flow activities of their choice, talk about what equipment is available and how it should be used for their own and other's safety.

Continue to develop these skills by providing interesting activities that require a range of **fine motor** skills e.g. set a challenge day such as making a bridge out of paper that will take the weight of a plastic person or animal.

Additional activities

These are additional activities to further support this stage of development.

Shoot to score

Chalk targets on walls and floors. Children take it in turns to kick or throw balls at wall targets or to throw bean bags at floor targets while keeping a score by adding totals or keeping a tally chart. Adjust the numbers used depending on children's mathematical abilities.

Basket ball

Set up a basket ball hoop and provide a range of different-sized balls for shooting practice. Vary the height as children become more confident and capable.

Skittle alley

Encourage children to make their own skittles using cardboard tubes which they decorate and number.

Arrange in a skittle pattern for children to knock down using different-sized balls and from varying distances. Play a tournament to find your champion skittler.

Baking day

Make pizzas and bread rolls. Encourage children to use whole hand knuckles and fingers to push, pull and pat whilst kneading the dough. Teach safe use of cutlery when spreading pizza toppings and buttering the rolls.

Musical masterpiece

Chose a 'conductor' and give him/her a selection of cards with words and symbols for loud, quiet, fast and slow. A small group of children choose musical instruments and follow the 'conductor' as they create a musical masterpiece.

Wacky racers

Set a challenge for children to construct their own vehicles and race them. Sometimes the practitioner or children choose specific construction sets or equipment that can be used. Other times let their imagination run wild and allow them to select freely from the environment

Left to it

Be aware of children who may be left-handed or still undecided about hand dominance. Make sure you provide a range of left-handed tools, such as scissors (ensure they are really left-handed and the blade is reversed with the left blade on the top so that the cutting line can be seen and a lean cut achieved). Be aware of how you set up resources. Can they be accessed equally from both sides?

Swing time

Encourage the use of monkey bars for swinging and developing upper body strength.

Glossary of terms

Visual perception: interpreting the surroundi environment using sight.

Spatial awareness: the recognition of the distance between objects and then ability to judge where you are in relation to objects.

Core stability: the muscle group (including abdominals) responsible for stabilising the body and supporting posture

Gross motor: the larger movements of arms, legs, feet or the entire body (including crawling, running, rolling, pulling up and jumping)

Fine motor: Movements that require a high degree of control and precision. These may include drawing, writing, cutting with scissors , using cutlery.

Manipulative skills: motor skills that involve using an object

Early Years Outcomes

Shows a preference for a dominant hand.

Begins to use anti-clockwise movement and retrace vertical lines.

Links to the Characteristics of Effective Learning

PLAYING AND EXPLORING

Finding out and exploring

★ using senses to explore the world around them

★ engaging in open-ended activity

Being willing to have a go

★ seeking challenge

★ showing a 'can do' attitude

★ taking a risk, engaging in new experiences, learning by trial and error

e.g. the child will continue to practise swirling movements with ribbons on sticks until they create the circular pattern they wish to achieve. They will notice which movements cause the ribbons to tangle and which movements are smoother. The practitioner can model different ways of moving both ribbon sticks at the same time and in different patterns to increase the challenge for the child.

ACTIVE LEARNING

Being involved and concentrating

★ showing high levels of energy, fascination

Keeping on trying

★ persisting with an activity when challenges occur

Enjoying achieving what they set out to do

★ showing satisfaction in meeting their own goals

e.g. the child will focus their attention on aiming the bean bags into the hoops and will keep trying to reach the central hoop. The practitioner can increase the challenge by encouraging the child to use a different hand when throwing or by standing further away.

CREATING AND THINKING CRITICALLY

Having their own ideas

★ finding new ways to do things

e.g. the child discovers that it is easier to use one hand for pouring or cutting.

Observation
What you may notice...

Does the child swap tools from hand to hand mid use?

Does the child change hands depending on the activity being **fine** or **gross motor**?

Can the child draw or copy anti-clockwise circles or retrace vertical lines independently in their own mark making play?

Assessment
What it may signify...

Unaware of **mid-line** of body, hand dominance not established.

Gross motor coordination needs to be established before working on **fine motor** skills.

The child is developing good **hand-eye coordination** and is choosing to explore the patterns and shapes linked to early writing through their play.

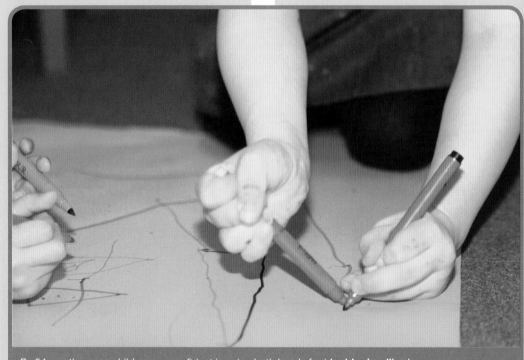

*By 54 months many children are confident in using both hands for '**double doodling**'.*

Planning
What you can do...

This links to sections 8 and 9 of the Progress Checklist on p86.

Encourage '**double doodle**' activities with a crayon or paintbrush in each hand, use both at the same time on both a large and small scale; play circle games passing an object from hand to hand and then around the circle

Play aiming, throwing and catching games with balloons, large balls or bean bags, noting which hand is used

With ribbon streamers, show the child how to trace an infinity symbol (∞) in the air. Always start the movement from the bottom right and move up through to the top left in a continuous flow. Swap hands when the child is confident with the pattern of movement. This activity exercises the **gross motor** muscles in preparation for future **fine motor** control. The right through to left movement reflects the correct direction for forming most letters.

By 54 months many children are able to move rhythmically to a range of music.

Additional activities

These are additional activities to further support this stage of development.

Note: **For all of the suggested activities, allow the child to choose which hand leads. For those children who have not yet established hand dominance, encourage them to try with both.**

Bean bag game

Play the bean bag game using in a bucket outside. Can the child pick up the blue bean bag and throw it into the bucket with their right hand? Try the green bean bag with the left? Model underarm throw.

Hand songs

Sing songs relating to left and right hands and encourage children to wave the correct hand e.g. 'Wave your right hand in the air, in the air…' (To the tune of *If you're happy and you know it*).

Puppets

Let the children play with puppets on left and right hands – give each a name and create a story about 'Rosie Right' and Leo Left', encouraging the child to move the correct puppet in time with the story.

Tray game

Play the tray game with a range of small objects. Ask the child to pick up the wooden peg with their right hand; pick up the marble with their left hand etc. This activity also encourages use of a pincer grip.

Pasta jewels

Allow the children to thread pasta tubes using string and wool to create their own necklaces. Toss the dry pasta in a tray of food colouring and leave to dry overnight for extra variety. The children may like to add glitter and gems using a 'sticky finger' technique (one finger acts as glue spreader).

Growing independence

Encourage and support the child as they learn to fasten and unfasten buttons, zips, buckles and laces. Have a range of doll or teddy bear clothes that they can play with to practise these key self-care skills. Ensure that popular role play clothes suited to both genders include a range c fastenings.

Tidy up time

Allow the children to take responsibility for tidying up at the end of each session. Let them wash th paint pots or snack plates and dry them using a tea towel or old cloth. Have small brushes for them to sweep up sand and dustpans and brushes to scoop it into the bin. Encourage them to put toys and counters back into their storage jars, so they can practise the skill of screwing an unscrewing lids on plastic jars.

Cutting practice

Use blunt or plastic scissors to cut and snip at a lump of dough, progressing to a block of clay for more resistance.

Glossary of terms

Mid line: refers to the imaginary line that divide the body into right and left halves.

Gross motor: larger movements of arms, legs feet, or the entire body (including crawling, runn rolling, pulling up and jumping).

Fine motor: movements that require a high degree of control and precision. These may inclu drawing, writing, cutting with scissors, using cutlery.

Hand-eye coordination: ability to use the eyes and hands together to perform an activity, for example, stringing beads, completing puzzle playing board games

Double doodle: this is a Brain Gym® movem that involves the use of both hands and draws awareness to the mid line of the body. With a lar sheet of paper or in the air with ribbon sticks, dr simple shapes and doodles with both hands at same time. Start in the middle and move up and out. Repeat patterns with different colours.

arly Years Outcomes

Begins to form recognisable letters.

Uses a pencil and holds it effectively to form recognisable letters, most of which are correctly formed.

nks to the Characteristics of Effective Learning

PLAYING AND EXPLORING

Finding out and exploring

★ using senses to explore the world around them

★ engaging in open-ended activity

Being willing to have a go

★ seeking challenge

★ showing a 'can do' attitude

★ taking a risk, engaging in new experiences, learning by trial and error

e.g. the child may explore letter formation and refine their fine motor skills through multiple sensory activities e.g. drawing shapes in the mud with a stick, tracing letters in custard with their fingers. They will respond to new experiences with excitement and curiosity and will transfer and apply letter formation skills in different contexts.

ACTIVE LEARNING

Being involved and concentrating

★ showing high levels of energy, fascination

Keeping on trying

★ persisting with activities when challenges occur

Enjoying achieving what they set out to do

★ showing satisfaction in meeting their own goals

e.g. the child may become engrossed in the repetition of letter shapes and mark making patterns and choose to practise these skills for an extended period of time. They may find some letters challenging and will keep trying, sometimes with adult support and encouragement. The child will show pride in their achievements and wish to share their success with key adults.

CREATING AND THINKING CRITICALLY

Having their own ideas

★ finding new ways to do things

e.g. the child will choose to practice their fine motor control and letter formation using different materials and on a range of surfaces. It is important that the practitioner provides a wide range of mark making tools and equipment for the child to access independently.

40 – 60+ months

LETTERS

PENCIL CONTROL

Observation
What you may notice…

Can the child form recognisable letters e.g. from their name?

Does the child pick up pencils and mark making tools and hold them correctly using the **tripod grasp**?

Can the child form letters correctly that have been modelled, including those linked to letters and sounds they have learned?

Assessment
What it may signify…

The child is establishing good **gross motor** coordination and is now working on developing their **fine motor** skills.

The child is developing good **fine motor** skills and can hold pencils and writing tools correctly using their thumb, index finger and middle finger in the **tripod grasp**.

The child is developing the correct **posture** and **fine motor** physical movements for letter formation. Their awareness of their physical **mid-line** is developing, enabling them to cross this as part of the writing process.

Planning
What you can do...

This links to sections 10 and 11 of the Progress Checklist on p86.

Explore name writing and recognition through a variety of sensory experiences. Go on a name hunt in the outdoor area; trace letters using the index finger on the carpet or in **gloop**. Use tablet devices to trace letters using fingers.

Use a **vertical** surface (e.g. easel or external wall) for **fine motor** activities such as painting and chalking. Form large letter shapes repeatedly in patterns of different colours. This will allow the child to feel the correct formation with their **gross motor** and **fine motor** muscles.

- When the child is ready for correct letter formation, ensure they are seated with their back to the chair back, all chair legs securely anchored on the floor and both of their feet facing forwards. Position the paper so that it is in front of their body and central to them (for right- handed children) or with their body slightly to the right and the paper angled slightly to the right at the bottom (for left-handed children).

- Model how writing flows from left to right and encourage a relaxed pincer grasp and a whole – arm movement. An A4 ring binder can be used as an alternative to a sloping table if the child requires some height to help with their posture and pencil control.

Positioning paper for left-handed writer

Additional activities

These are additional activities to further support this stage of development.

Lazy 8s

This is a **Brain Gym**® movement that encourages the correct posture and physical movements for future letter formation. It is called 'Lazy 8s' as the infinity symbol looks like the number 8 having a rest and lying down! Provide the child with a large template of the infinity symbol securely fastened to an easel or taped to the table. Using a crayon or pencil in their dominant hand, encourage the child to trace over the shape repeatedly (again, starting bottom right flowing through to top left and back around).

Keyboard games

Use a piano or keyboard to build individual finger strength. Place coloured stickers on each key and on the child's fingers. Can they press the coloured key with the same coloured finger? Do the same activity with a computer keyboard or allow the children to word process through typing random letters in their play. Link to role play activities as a musician or an administrator.

Round and round we go!

Provide different-shaped and coloured pieces of paper and a range of stencils linked to a theme or topic for the children to draw around. Can they hold the stencil with one hand whilst they draw around the edge with the other? Further develop **fine motor** control by encouraging the child to cut out their stencilled shape and colour it in. Remember to provide appropriate scissors for left-handed children.

My name is...

Have a range of magnetic letters on the table. Can the child find the letters that make up their name? Use letters cut from fine sandpaper for the child to trace over with their index finger, then place their letters under paper and use wax crayons to run over the textured surface. Provide laminated name cards for the child to use to model the letters in their name. Allow them to explore copying or tracing these with a range of mark making tools including large paintbrushes and water outside. Encourage the child to write their name on their art work and other things to go home, so name – writing has a purpose.

Spray fun

Spray or paint large circular shapes and lines outside using water.

Tracing with a purpose

Cut pieces of tracing paper or good quality baking parchment and leave near a range of clearly illustrated books (e.g. *Kipper* by Mick Inkpen). Provide small bulldog clips for the children to squeeze as they clip their tracing paper on to the page they wish to copy. Encourage them to follow the outlines with care before removing their tracing paper and colouring in their creation! The more independently the child can do this, the stronger and more refined their **fine motor skills** become.

Letter families

In terms of letter formation, the letter families listed below follow similar movement patterns and it can be useful to allow children to practise forming these as a group. First approach letter formation in a multi-sensory way before moving on to pencil and paper methods. Explore forming letters outside with ropes on the floor, with powder paint in puddles, in wet sand using mini people to push through, in mud or snow with a stick or in porridge with a spoon. Whichever malleable materials you have in your setting, letter formation can be a part of that play and exploration. When the child is ready for pencil and paper formation, model the correct starting point for each letter and the formation pattern.

Curly caterpillar:
c a d o s g q e f

Long ladder:
l i t u j y

One-arm robot:
r b n h m k p

Zig-zag monster:
z v w x

By 54 months many children are able to select individual **digits** to press into dough or clay.

Glossary of terms

Tripod grasp (on writing implement): three fingered; thumb, index, and middle fingers.

Gross motor: is the coordination and control of the large muscle groups and relate to whole body movement. They develop in infancy in a head to toe order.

Fine motor: movements that require a high degree of control and precision. These may include drawing, writing, cutting with scissors, using cutlery.

Posture: a particular position of the body.

Mid line: refers to the imaginary line that divides the body into right and left halves.

Gloop: cornflour and water mixed to varying consistencies

Vertical: a line in space going from top to bottom or bottom to top.

Pincer grip: grasping an object between the thumb and forefinger. The ability to perform this task is a milestone of fine motor development in infants, usually occurring from 9 to 12 months of age.

Brain Gym®: a group of body-based movement tools developed by Paul Dennison for advancing learning skills.

Digit: a human finger or toe.

Progress Checklist: 40 – 60 months

Name ....

Date						
Age in months						

Use different coloured pens to track assessments so that progress can be seen.

Tick 'yes' if the child is fully able to perform the movement.

Tick 'some difficulty' if the child can sometimes perform the movement but not easily.

Tick 'severe difficulty' if the child rarely or never performs the movement.

Early Learning Goal - children show good control and coordination in large and small movements. They move confidently, in a range of ways, negotiating space. They handle equipment and tools effectively, including pencils for writing.

		Yes	Some difficulty	Severe difficulty
1a	Able to demonstrate different ways of travelling. (Note different ways seen e.g. running, skipping, hopping, crawling, rolling)			
2a	Able to jump from a low object and land on two feet.			
3a	Able to change direction to avoid collision when moving quickly.			
3b	Able to adjust their speed to avoid obstacles.			
4a	Able to travel skillfully under, over and through equipment.			
5a	Able to throw a ball to another child. (Note size of ball, accuracy and which hand they use or if it is both)			
5b	Able to catch a ball when thrown directly to them. (Note size of ball)			
5c	Able to kick a ball to someone. (Note accuracy and which foot they use)			
6a	Able to manipulate and change materials using simple tools.			
7a	Able to use scissors safely.			
7b	Able to cut out simple shapes independently.			
8a	Consistently shows preference for the same hand. (Note which)			
9a	Able to use anticlockwise movements and retrace vertical lines. (If just one, note which)			
10a	Able to form some recognisable letters. (Note which ones)			
11a	Able to pick up pencils and mark making tools using a tripod grasp.			
11b	Able to form some letters correctly. (Note which ones)			

*Many of these can be watched on YouTube

Buzzy Bee

Here comes the buzzy bee, buzz, buzz, buzz;

(fly into sight from left to right)

Where is the buzzy bee? Buzz, buzz, buzz.

(fly out of sight, repeat from other direction and as often from both sides as child remains interested.)

Here we go round the mulberry bush*

Here we go round the mulberry bush,
The mulberry bush,
The mulberry bush.
Here we go round the mulberry bush
On a cold and frosty morning.

This is the way we wash our face…

This is the way we comb our hair…

This is the way we stamp our feet…

(Repeat as many times as you like with different actions)

Dingle Dangle Scarecrow

When all the cows were sleeping and the sun had gone to bed
Up jumped the scarecrow and this is what he said!
'I'm a dingle, dangle scarecrow with a flippy floppy hat,
I can shake my hands like this and shake my feet like that.'

When all the hens were roosting and the moon behind the cloud
Up jumped the scarecrow and shouted very loud:
'I'm a dingle, dangle scarecrow with a flippy floppy hat,
I can shake my hands like this and shake my feet like that.'

When the dogs were in the kennels and the doves were in the loft
Up jumped the scarecrow and whispered very soft:
'I'm a dingle, dangle scarecrow with a flippy floppy hat,
I can shake my hands like this and shake my feet like that.'

Hokey Cokey*

You put your left arm in,
Your left arm out
In, out, in, out,
You shake it all about.
You do the hokey cokey and you turn around
That's what it's all about.

[Chorus]

Woah, the hokey cokey,
Woah, the hokey cokey,
Woah, the hokey cokey,
Knees bent, arms stretched, ra ra ra!

You put your right arm in,
Your right arm out
In, out, in, out,
You shake it all about.
You do the hokey cokey and you turn around
That's what it's all about...

(Repeat chorus)

You put your left leg in...

(Repeat chorus)

You put your right leg in...

(Repeat chorus)

You put your whole self in...

(Repeat chorus)

Horsey horsey*

Horsie, horsie don't you stop,
Just let your feet go clippety clop,
Your tail goes swish and the wheels go round,
Giddy up we're homeward bound.

Steady Neddy off you trot,
Just let your feet go clippety clop,
Your tail goes swish and the wheels go round,
Giddy up we're off to town.

Hop little bunnies*

See the little bunnies sleeping till it's nearly noon
Shall we go and wake them with a merry tune?
They're so still... are they ill?
Wake up little bunnies!

Hop little bunnies, hop, hop, hop
Hop, hop, hop - hop, hop, hop
Hop little bunnies, hop, hop, hop
Hop, hop, hop... (and repeat)

In and out the dusty bluebells*

In and out the dusty bluebells,
In and out the dusty bluebells,
In and out the dusty bluebells,
Who will be my master?

Tippy-tappy tippy-tappy
On my shoulder.............
Tippy-tappy tippy-tappy
On my shoulder.............
Tippy-tappy tippy-tappy
On my shoulder.............
You will be my master.

Songs and rhymes

Jack and Jill*

*Jack and Jill went up the hill
To fetch a pail of water.
Jack fell down and broke his crown,
And Jill came tumbling after.
Up Jack got and home did trot,
As fast as he could caper;
And went to bed and bound his head
With vinegar and brown paper.*

Jack in the box

*Jack in the box, Jack in the box
Curl up small
Jack in the box, Jack in the box
Jump up tall!*

Make the bed

*Make the bed
Shake the bed
Turn the blanket over!*

One, two, three, four, five*

(linked to touching fingers and toes)

*One, two, three, four, five,
Once I caught a fish alive,
Six, seven, eight, nine, ten,
Then I let it go again.*

*Why did you let it go?
Because it bit my finger so.
Which finger did it bite?
This little finger on the right.*

(Can be repeated with different sea creatures replacing the fish).

Ring a rosies*

*Ring-a-ring o' roses,
A pocket full of posies,
A-tishoo! A-tishoo!
We all fall down.*

Tommy Thumb*

*Tommy Thumb, Tommy Thumb,
Where are you?
Here I am, here I am,
How do you do?*

(Wiggle your index finger)

*Peter Pointer, Peter Pointer,
Where are you?
Here I am, here I am,
How do you do?*

(Wiggle your middle finger)

*Toby Tall, Toby Tall,
Where are you?
Here I am, here I am,
How do you do?*

(Wiggle the fourth finger)

*Ruby Ring, Ruby Ring,
Where are you?
Here I am, here I am,
How do you do?*

(Wiggle the the littlest finger of all)

*Baby Small, Baby Small,
Where are you?
Here I am, here I am,
How do you do?*

(Put all of your fingers in the air, give them a wiggle and wave them everywhere)

*Fingers all, Fingers all,
Where are you?
Here we are, here we are,
How do you do?
Here we are, here we are,
How do you do?*

Rock–a–bye baby*

Rock-a-bye baby, in the treetop
When the wind blows, the cradle will rock
When the bough breaks, the cradle will fall
And down will come baby, cradle and all.

Round and round the garden*

Round and round the garden
Like a teddy bear.
One step, two step,
Tickle you under there!
Round and round the garden
In the pouring rain.
One step, two step
Tickle you there again!

Row your boat*

Row, row, row your boat
Gently down the stream
Merrily, merrily, merrily, merrily
Life is but a dream!

Row, row, row your boat
Gently up the creek
If you see a little mouse
Don't forget to squeak!

Row, row, row your boat
Gently down the stream
If you see a crocodile
Don't forget to scream!

Row, row, row your boat
Gently to the shore
If you see a lion
Don't forget to roar!

Skip to my Lou*

Skip, skip, skip to my Lou, (x3)
Skip to my Lou, my darlin'.
(Sing changing verse here, repeated 3 times)
Skip to my Lou, my darlin'.

The changing verse

- *Fly's in the buttermilk, Shoo, fly, shoo*
- *There's a little red wagon, Paint it blue*
- *Lost my partner, What'll I do?*
- *I'll get another one, Prettier than you*
- *Can't get a red bird, Jay bird'll do*
- *Cat's in the cream jar, Ooh, ooh, ooh*

Teddy bear, teddy bear

Teddy bear, teddy bear turn around,
Teddy bear, teddy bear, touch the ground
Teddy bear, teddy bear, curl up small
Teddy bear, teddy bear, stand up tall…
Teddy bear, teddy bear turn around,
Teddy bear, teddy bear, touch the ground
Teddy bear, teddy bear, switch off the light
Teddy bear, teddy bear, say goodnight!

Ten in the bed*

*There were ten in the bed
And the little one said,
"Roll over, roll over"
So they all rolled over and one fell out!
(repeat with each number in reverse until there
is one in the bed…)*

*There was one in the bed
And the little one said,
"Goodnight!"*

The Grand Old Duke of York*

*Oh, the Grand Old Duke of York,
He had ten thousand men,
He marched them up to the top of the hill
And he marched them down again.
And when they were up they were up.
And when they were down they were down.
And when they were only half way up,
They were neither up nor down.*

This little piggy*

*This little piggy went to the market,
This little piggy stayed home,
This little piggy had roast beef,
This little piggy had none,
And this little piggy cried 'wee wee wee'
All the way to town!*

Wind the Bobbin up*

*Wind the bobbin up (x2)
Pull, pull, clap, clap, clap
Wind the bobbin up (x2)
Pull, pull, clap, clap, clap
Point to the ceiling, point to the floor
Point to the window, point to the door
Clap your hands together, one two three,
Put your hands upon your knee.*

*Wind it back again (x2)
Pull, pull, clap, clap, clap
Wind it back again (x2)
Pull, pull, clap, clap, clap
Point to the ceiling, point to the floor
Point to the window, point to the door
Clap your hands together, one two three,
Put your hands upon your knee.*

TNR: Asymmetrical Tonic Neck Reflex. This is a rimitive reflex usually present up to 6 months. It is een when the child is lying on their back and their ead is turned to one side. On the same side that ne head is facing, the arm should reach out and ne leg straighten. The arm and leg on the opposite de should bend. This is sometimes known as ne 'fencer' position. It supports the development f hand/eye coordination, and the motor skills of eading, rolling, crawling and standing.

abinski reflex: this is a primitive reflex which ccurs after the sole of the foot has been firmly troked up the outside edge of the sole and along ne pads beneath the toes. The big toe then moves pward or toward the top surface of the foot. The ther toes fan out. This reflex is normal in children o to 2 years old. It disappears as the child gets der.

Babinski reflex

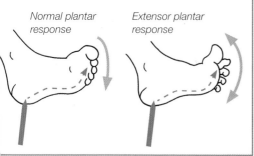
Normal plantar response *Extensor plantar response*

rain Gym®: a group of body-based movement ools developed by Paul Dennison Phd for dvancing learning skills. 101 course — a 4 day oundation course for Educational Kinesiology hich demonstrates how to apply the Brain Gym® novements. For further details visit ww.braingym.org.uk

ommentating: speaking out loud about what ou notice the child doing whilst you play alongside nem. This provides them with new vocabulary and nodels correct speech.

ore stability: the muscle group (including bdominals) responsible for stabilising the body nd supporting posture.

ore strength: the ability to use tummy and back nuscles in a balanced way.

Cross lateral: a movement that crosses the mid line of the body—right hand and left foot together, left hand and right foot together.

Digit: a human finger or toe.

Dominant hand: the hand a child regularly and instinctively uses for fine motor control activities.

Double doodle: this is a Brain Gym® movement that involves the use of both hands and draws awareness to the mid line of the body. With a large sheet of paper or in the air with ribbon sticks, draw simple shapes and doodles with both hands at the same time. Start in the middle and move up and out. Repeat patterns with different colours.

Enclosing: the child explores building 3D enclosures using blocks or bricks or creates 2D border by putting lines around their paintings or drawings.

Eye tracking: the movement of the eyes when following and object.

Fine motor: movements that require a high degree of control and precision. These may include drawing, writing, cutting with scissors, using cutlery.

Gait: a technical term for walking.

Gloop: corn flour and water mixed to varying consistencies.

Grasping: the child explores handling a range of objects in different sensory situations (e.g. slippery, dry, cold, warm).

Gross motor skills: the use of large muscle groups such as those in the arms, legs and core to support a range of physical activities including crawling, rolling, pulling up and walking. They develop in infancy in a head to toe order.

Gross motor: the larger movements of arms, legs, feet or the entire body (including crawling, running, rolling, pulling up and jumping).

Hand-eye coordination: ability to use the eyes and hands together to perform an activity, for example, stringing beads, completing puzzles, playing board games.

Head righting reflex: when the head is not in an upright position, this reflex stimulates appropriate muscles to bring it back into an upright position.

Hip flexion: when the hip moves the limb forwards towards the front of the body.

Hip rotation: when the hip turns the limb inwards or outwards.

Homolateral: a one sided movement—left hand and foot together then right hand and foot together.

Horizontal: relating to the horizon, e.g. a line going from left to right.

Integrated reflex: when the reflex has served its purpose in supporting an area of development.

Manipulative skills: motor skills that involve using an object.

Mentally process: to think things through.

Mid line: refers to the imaginary line that divides the body into right and left halves.

Motor skills: relating to physical movement (see gross and fine motor skills).

Muscle resistant play: heavy work and proprioceptive play activities that provide resistance so that muscle strength is developed.

Muscle tone: an unconscious low level contraction of muscles at rest.

Non-dominant: the arm/hand or leg/foot that the child does not usually choose to use for kicking a ball, handling tools etc.

Palmar grip/grasp: using the whole hand to hold onto and use objects.

Palmar reflex: a primitive reflex that curls the fingers when the palm of the hand is tickled, also known as the 'grasp' reflex. This reflex exercises th hand muscles and supports fine motor control.

Pincer grip: grasping an object between the thum and forefinger. The ability to perform this task is a milestone of fine motor development in infants, usually occurring from 9 to 12 months of age.

Pitch: how high or low a musical note or sound is.

Plantar reflex: a primitive reflex which occurs afte the pads beneath the toes on the sole of the foot have been firmly pressed. In children/adults above years of age the toes curve down and inwards, this is a healthy response.

Positioning: the child explores putting objects in particular positions (e.g. in lines, behind or under things).

Posture: a particular position of the body.

Propel: to cause to move forwards or onwards.

Proprioceptive feedback: sensory feedback tha tells us where our body parts are in space without having to look. e.g. being able to put an object into our mouth. It also helps us to know how much fore we need to use to do something e.g. how hard to grip something without squashing it or how to throw a ball so that it goes far enough but not too far. Activities involving resistance give us the most feedback.

Schema: a repeated pattern of behaviour which supports a child in their exploratiion and understanding of their world. These may include: grasping, positioning, transporting and enclosing.

Sensory exploration: using the senses to make sense of the world.

Spatial awareness: the recognition of the distanc between objects and the ability to judge where yo are in relation to objects.

STNR: Symmetrical Tonic Neck Reflex. This reflex usually integrates at 9-12 months. It supports the development of crawling, pulling to standing posit and walking. This reflex is normal in children up to years old. It disappears as the child gets older.

actile: affecting the sense of touch.

ansporting: the child explores moving objects om one place to another, sometimes using a asket, wheelbarrow or pushchair.

ipod grip: (on objects): thumb, index, and middle ngers; less mature than pincer grasp.

ipod grasp: (on writing implement): three ngered; thumb, index, and middle fingers.

pper and lower gross motor muscles: the rger muscles in the arms and legs.

ertical: a line in space going from top to bottom or ottom to top.

Visual skills: the ability to perceive what is seen.

Visual midfield: the area that both eyes can see at the same time.

Visual perception: interpreting the surrounding environment using eye sight.

Visual spatial relations: the ability to recognise a shape, object, or letter when presented in different positions, for example, puzzles, block designs.

Visual stimuli: something that provokes a response from the eyes e.g. a picture, toy or object.

Volume: how loud or quiet a musical note or sound is.

Tripod grip

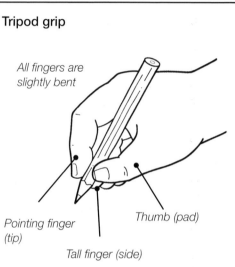

All fingers are slightly bent

Pointing finger (tip)

Thumb (pad)

Tall finger (side)

Don't do this!

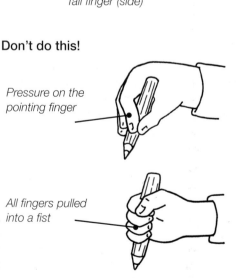

Pressure on the pointing finger

All fingers pulled into a fist

Statutory Framework for the Early Years
Department for Education
www.education.gov.uk/publications/standard/
AllPublications/Page1/DFE-00023-2012
(Information from this publication used under the
terms of the Open Government Licence
www.nationalarchives.gov.uk/doc/open-
government-licence/)

Early Years Outcomes
Department for Education
Reference: DFE-00167-2013
(Information from this publication used under the
terms of the Open Government Licence v2.0
www.nationalarchives.gov.uk)

Development Matters
Early Education
www.early-education.org.uk
(Information from this publication used under the
terms of the Open Government Licence v2.0)

Steps of Development From Birth to Four
Ernst J.Kiphard
Borgmann Publishing Ltd.
978-1-8549-2012-6

Understanding the Revised Early Years Foundation Stage
Helen Moylett and Nancy Stewart
Early Education
978–0–9041–8758-8

Movement and Learning
Wombat and his Mates Song Book and CD
Brendan O'Hara
The F# Music Company
0-9751138-0-1

Mary Sheridan's From Birth to Five Years Children's Developmental Progress Fourth Edition
Ajay Sharma and Helen Cockerill
Routledge
978-0-415-83354-7

Practical EYFS Handbook
Penny Tassoni
Heinemann
978-0-43589-991-2

Motor Skills Development A teaching/parents' guide and children's activity book
Downloadable PDF
www.staidenshomeschool.com
© 2009 Donnette E. Davis. All Rights Reserved.

www.drawyourworld.com/blog/hold-the-pencil.htr
Information on guiding children to use the correct
pencil grip.